Teach to learn

Learn to teach

by

Berwick Coates

Published by Berwick Coates

Publishing partner: Paragon Publishing, Rothersthorpe

© Berwick Coates 2022

The rights of Berwick Coates to be identified as the author of this work have been asserted by him in accordance with the Copyright, Designs and Patents Act of 1988.

All rights reserved; no part of this publication may be reproduced, stored in a retrieval system, or transmitted in any form or by any means, electronic, mechanical, photocopying, recording or otherwise without the prior written consent of the publisher or a licence permitting copying in the UK issued by the Copyright Licensing Agency Ltd. www.cla.co.uk

ISBN 978-1-78222-950-6

Cover design by Stephen Goodwin – sgssdesign.co.uk

Book design, layout and production management by Into Print
www.intoprint.net
+44 [0]1604 832149

Dedication

To all those who
help us to learn

Introduction

WHAT ARE MY CREDENTIALS for holding forth like this?

I hold an honours degree in History from Cambridge University. My teaching diploma from London University included a Distinction in the Practical Examination.

I spent over forty years in the classroom, during which time I taught both sexes, all ages from seven to nineteen, all abilities from Remedial to Oxbridge entrance, and in pretty well every type of school – Primary, Secondary Modern, Grammar, Comprehensive, and Public School. I have wide experience in talking to adult audiences of every occupation from Army NCO and pensioner to undertaker and president of the International Guild of Knot Tyers. I have been a careers adviser, drama producer, and games coach. I have taught History, English, General Studies, Latin, and Swahili – three of them up to 'A' Level.

I have published nineteen books, over half of them connected with education.

I have given about 40,000 lessons.

Prologue

I SHOULD MAKE CLEAR, at the outset, that nearly everything I say from now on is about the whole, general business of teaching. It is not about becoming a teacher of French, or Maths, or English, or any subject in particular. It is not about teaching abroad, or teaching handicapped children, or teaching in deprived areas, or private tuition, or any specialised teaching activity. It is about teaching full stop. I simply hope that you might find it of use.

I should also like to make clear that nothing that follows constitutes a set of rules, or principles, or instructions, or formulas. There are no easy cribs or short cuts to make teaching easy. It isn't. There are no ten commandments of teaching.

I certainly do not want you to follow what I say simply because I say it, even if it appears to be smart or slick or impressive. However much you may be overawed by my ponderous credentials or vast experience or fathomless wisdom, keep your wits and gumption in full flow at all times. No matter how much sense it may have made to me in the past, it has to make sense to you now, or you won't be able to make it work. It would seem reasonable that you should give me credit for my qualifications and my record, but always keep your own judgment as a strategic reserve.

Put another way, if you don't buy it, you won't be able to sell it.

My guess is that most of what I have to say will be of more potential use to beginner teachers than to those with some service under their belts. Those latter performers will already be familiar with some of the best teaching practice; they will have absorbed the main features of a sound teacher attitude. Nevertheless, there may be sections or paragraphs or single remarks here that will cause them to think 'that's an idea', or 'worth a try', or 'I hadn't thought of looking at it like that before'. None of us knows everything.

One crumb of comfort to sustain you on your way: to do with nerves.

Teaching is difficult. Well, so what? If you think about it, everything is difficult. Proper performance demands care and concentration – driving a car, crossing the road, carving the Sunday joint, walking down the stairs. You can't afford *not* to concentrate, can you?

Everything becomes that much more difficult if you are coming to it for the first time. Especially teaching. Why? Because it is going flat against your whole life experience up to that point. From your first conscious moments you have been on the receiving end of education of one kind or another. Now, for the very first time, you are going to be dishing it out. A complete reversal of roles. That is daunting.

For perhaps the first time in your life, a group of more than a handful of human beings is going to be listening to what you have to say. Worse, you have to find a way of persuading them to go on listening, even if they would rather not be there.

Of course it is daunting. Of course you are nervous. Who wouldn't be? You are the most un-unique person on the planet. Do not add to your problems by tormenting yourself for *being* nervous. You are not odd. There is nothing wrong with being nervous. Coming in and performing a lesson for the first time is enough to worry anybody. As a matter of fact, nerves help you to do that; nerves give you that shot of adrenalin usually considered helpful for an energetic performance. And if there is a smart alec out there who thinks that the whole business is just about memorising some knowledge and talking about it, and that nerves and performance don't come into it, he has a lot to learn about teaching.

Gather up your nerves, then, slide them into your briefcase or your handbag, and use them if necessary for that shot of energy. Don't be ashamed of them, but don't parade them either, like battle scars.

Live with them, but don't let them get you down. I repeat: it is no sin to have nerves. But it is a little ill-advised to do nothing to control them. Perhaps some of the suggestions in this book may help you to do that.

Some of them may be mere tips, tiny points, random observations, which either you didn't know about or which had never occurred to you before. Simple and obvious. As I have already said, nobody knows everything, and we all have our blind spots.

Others may challenge an opinion you have held for some time, so you may need to search your mind to find good reasons to vindicate what you have been doing, or be prepared to give way to a superior argument. Either way, it could be good for you.

Or again, it could be an example of the old story of the traveller in Ireland who wanted to get directions to reach the next town up the road. He approached a venerable local inhabitant who looked both cheerful and willing to talk. The patriarch listened attentively with bowed head, which he wagged frequently to show that he understood completely the traveller's problem.

'Indeed, sorr. Indeed indeed. So it's Ballybungay you'll be after lookin' for. Ah, well, now, there's many a walker's been faced with a problem just like yours, and I wish I had a pound for every time I've been asked that question. It's happy I am to be able to give you the benefit of my experience. Well, if I were yourself, sorr, I wouldn't start from here at all, at all.' [With apologies for the hoary clichés.]

In other words, the problem may lie in the simple fact that you are coming at it from the wrong side altogether. It's not the detail, or the difficulty; it's the angle.

Contents

Dedication 3
Introduction 4
Prologue 5
1 Teaching small 10
2 Good manners 20
3 Good practices 30
4 Breaking the flow 40
5 Trouble in store 50
6 So now you're a teacher 61
7 Pious hopes 71
8 Scraps of solace 82
9 Asking questions 92
10 Teaching and trust 102
11 Professionalism in pupils 112
12 Putting yourself across 119
13 A good story 129
14 The debate on leadership 139
15 Classroom bureaucracy 149
16 Getting to know you 159
17 The question of bad pupils 166
18 Little bits of business 173
19 What to do with advice 180
20 A diversion 191
21 Thinking about teaching 195
22 Throwing the biscuit 209

1 Teaching small

LET US ASSUME THEN that you have picked up the hint dropped at the end of the Prologue, and that you have tumbled to the right approach to take; you know how to tackle it; you are coming at it from the right direction. Now what?

You make it as easy for yourself as you can, that's what. If the crate is heavy, you don't risk a hernia, do you? You move it bottle by bottle. You are tackling the problem, but in a manageable way. You are tackling it with greater confidence that you will succeed in solving it. And when you take on teaching, you can do with all the confidence you can get.

Don't think of it as one great big obstacle. Break it down. Or break it up, if you prefer. The smaller you make the pieces, the less daunting they become. If you think of a class as a giant creature with thirty heads, they can be frightening. Look at them as twenty-five or thirty individuals, and at once you have lessened the load. One for one, you'd back yourself against any of them, wouldn't you? Well then…

The next thing, obviously, is to start. Keep your formalities to a bare minimum. No fulsome, over-friendly greetings; no optimistic forecasts of happy partnerships; no detailed analysis of teaching programmes for weeks to come; no engaging little story to say how you came to the school. No. Business. Get on with it.

I once watched a television solo concert given by Frank Sinatra. All right, he was a great singer, and I was appropriately impressed. But the memory of that concert which stayed with me was his businesslike attitude. As I said, no fulsome greetings – 'how wonderful to be in your beautiful city' and all that; no fond reminiscences of the first time he had recorded that particular song; no sugary compliments about the artist who sang it with him twenty-seven years ago in some army camp six thousand miles away, just behind the lines. No. A formal entrance. A bow. A nod to the conductor of the orchestra, and he was away. When the song was over, a bow to the applause, then another nod to the conductor, and he was away again.

Singing was what he did best, so singing was what he did. The audience got its money's worth.

The same with teaching. Just start. And don't assault the whole house; take it brick by brick. What comes first?

Come in. That's right – come in. Make an entrance. Isn't that stupidly obvious? Not necessarily. It may depend on the way the school day, or the school geography, is organised, and you don't have any control over that. If you are tied to your classroom all day, and *they* come in to *you* every time, you are part of the furniture; while they settle down, gossip, and get out their books, they take no more notice of you than they do of the light bulbs.

But, if circumstances permit you to walk through the door and the class is there waiting for you, then take the opportunity – make an entrance.

I don't mean spring out of the floor in a puff of white smoke like the Demon King. I mean just come in, to a full room. They look up. They take notice. They can't help it. If you are new, even less can they help it. Either way, you are an event. You have influenced them. It's a start. You have the initiative.

When they leave at the end of the lesson, use the chance to make another entrance. If the school is so arranged that it is always the pupils who move, the timetable has to allow them to get from one room to another. That gives you the opportunity *not* to be part of the furniture. Put your head out for a couple of minutes of fresh air. Walk to the common room; the exercise will do you good. Change of pace; change of view; change of atmosphere. Cool off; calm down; freshen up; whatever. However brief, it gives you a break.

And when you come back, you can make an entrance all over again. If it's the children who stay put and the staff who move, then it's even easier; you *have to* make an entrance – four, five, six times or more every day. Every time you do that you are an event.

Again, you have the initiative. Hang on to it. Remember what their expectations are. That a teacher will come in and tell them to do something. Well, do so. But keep it small. Keep it easy. Be sure it is something you can make happen. Think of the bricks, not the wall.

If possible, keep them dangling just a little. They are expecting you to start teaching. If you ask one of them to shut the door, they will do it, if only to get a small detail out of the way, so that they can get on with the meat of the lesson.

Shut the door; open a window; move a chair; pull a curtain back. Get them to do things which are so minimally ordinary and routine that it does not occur to them to disobey. Already you are incorporating them into the mechanics of the lesson. They are waiting for the lesson to start. What they do not realise is that it already has.

They are obeying you, without being fully aware that you are taking charge. You have already begun the habit of obedience.

If you have a class you have never seen before, here is the chance for some more 'small' teaching. Their names.

Of course you have a list, but you have to tie their faces to their names. Another very manageable brick for the wall. I don't mean just checking to make sure they are there. To do that you don't even have to take your nose out of your mark book. I mean making contact, making an effect.

You can make quite a little meal of this. Ask them, obviously. But ask them direct, face to face, eye to eye. You don't have to stare or glare; the trick is to *avoid* looking as if you are trying to make an impression. Casual. Understated. Just look. But look thoroughly, steadily, as if you are trying to commit their faces to memory. Well, you are. But you are having an effect. A constant gaze for only two or three seconds is out of the normal. People only glance most of the time. We are not used to being well and truly looked at, however quietly.

You can go further. If the name is unusual, ask them to repeat it. Repeat it back to them, to confirm. If it is difficult, practise it with them, till you are sure and they are satisfied. Getting a name right is a sign of politeness. That carries weight too. Subconscious maybe. They don't say to themselves, 'This man has a healthy teacher attitude.' No. But politeness registers. They appreciate it.

Even make a comment if a suitable one occurs to you, but make sure it is complimentary. This question-and-answer session is going on in front of twenty or thirty people.

Whatever you are doing in all this, you are making contact. With every direct word and every direct glance, you are gaining creeping control. Every second eye to eye counts.

And it's easy so long as you concentrate. Concentration is catching, like the measles. If you do it, so will they.

I have heard several famous orchestral conductors say that one at least of the secrets of successful conducting is to do with eye contact. In the depths of that vortex of sawing and banging and blowing and arm-waving, what produces a great sound is the maestro's eye fixing the eye of the second trombonist just before the final *fortissimo*.

Many years ago, I watched a film of Arturo Toscanini (reckoned by many of his colleagues to be the greatest conductor of all) directing a huge choral work. One of the cameras was stationed immediately behind the choir. The orchestra was winding up a mighty crescendo prior to the climactic entry of the choir at the Great Moment. Toscanini was sharing his attention between the score and the orchestra, till the Great Moment came. He suddenly looked up to the choir, and we, the viewers, in the camera, as it were, caught the full force of the apocalyptic fire in the maestro's eye. I remember thinking that, if I, as a member of that choir, had missed the entry, at the very least the sky would have fallen in.

It is a pleasant thought that humble classroom teachers have that much in common with great orchestral conductors, in that, with a mere eye, they have the potential to produce similar moments of enlightenment, effort, and truth.

With the eye, then, you can do a lot of small teaching. You can also do a lot by letting it look as if you are doing practically nothing at all.

I have suggested giving tiny instructions – 'shut the door, please' – and asking tiny questions – 'What's your name?' You can also do tiny things.

Particularly useful, this, if you like moving while you are teaching. The question of movement is almost a whole topic in itself, and has no doubt exercised the intellects of many an educational psychologist and teaching guru.

I'm sure that plenty of justification can be offered for either. Have you ever thought about it? Are you a stander or a wanderer? A focus or a moving target? (Depending perhaps on how volatile the class is.)

Nor is there any reason for insisting that you should be the one or the other, permanently. Why not be either as your mood and the situation dictate? I am simply suggesting that movement can be conducive to the little technique I am about to describe.

It is all part of the 'kidology' of teaching. Its attractiveness lies in its simplicity and its sheer do-ability. We are back to the bricks and the wall again. Doing it small.

As you move about the classroom, you may see a stray glove on the floor. One reaction is to ignore it. No. You have missed an opportunity. Another is to pick it up, wave it about, and say 'Who owns this?' No again. It breaks the flow of what you are doing, and it breaks their concentration, which you have just spent twenty minutes building.

What do you do then? Without breaking the flow of your own words in any way, you bend, you pick it up, and you put it on the desk of the pupil who is sitting the nearest. You do not ask the pupil if it is theirs; you do not hold it up and ask the class who owns it. You make a complete non-event of it. Barely look at it. Certainly not refer back to it. The minute you move on – as you do – it ceases to exist.

So what have you done?

You have shown that you have maintained total control

and total continuity. You have exhibited no fuss whatever. You have shown that you have noticed something that, ideally, needed doing, you have done it, and, by moving on without reference to it, have demonstrated its level of importance in the general scheme of things. But you have shown that you are in sufficient control to notice something outside the lesson while not relaxing your grip *on* the lesson. You have been observant, and you have done something that may improve the welfare of a pupil in however tiny a way.

Children miss a lot, but they notice a lot too.

More tiny things? How about this? When you give out a set of exercise books you have just finished marking, how do you do it? Hand them over to a pupil to distribute? Well, yes, a time-honoured method. Always be aware of the value of Pupil Power. But no contact between teacher and pupil.

Or the casual technique – you know, the informal approach. Toss them across the room towards the individual owners. Always good for a chuckle or two. All very comradely. But ironic in that you, as a teacher, like to insist that they take care of school property, and here you are setting a questionable example by committing assault and battery on thirty books at a time, every week.

If you give out the books individually, it takes a bit longer, but, honestly, not all that much. But you gain in that individual contact again – face to face, eye to eye. You can talk briefly about what they have done – a good map, a promising paragraph, or on the other hand a snappy rebuke for yet another piece of sloppy work, which, as it is in front of the class, may induce a twinge of shame. Careful here, of course. There is a difference between savaging a piece of genuine work and proving that a particular page is demonstrably below normal standards accepted by one and all.

Given that you are careful in what you say, this can be invaluable, and it doesn't take long. And the pupil will do more than simply glance at the figure out of ten and sling it in the desk.

Teaching small – all these tiny things are easy to do, and they show that you take notice of detail. That you are on the ball. That you are in control. That you are interested in what they do. That you observe, that you listen, that you can talk. It can be cumulative, even exponential. Those dozens of little bricks you were able to deal with – unspectacularly, day in day out – you could wind up with quite an impressive wall after all. You have licked the wall.

Another great virtue of this approach is that it is not difficult to think of refinements of it. Any specialist will find ideas occurring to him which spring from the details and subtleties of his or her own subject. Each piece of 'small teaching' will be a potential success because it is just that – small and simple. The more success a teacher registers, the greater becomes his confidence, and therefore the sense of comfort. The more comfortable he becomes, the more comfortable he (please understand both 'he' and 'she'; I can't go on putting both every time) will appear to be. That means that his pupils become more comfortable too. Comfort is one of the most desirable conditions aimed for in one's everyday life.

Teaching small is not the be-all and end-all of teaching. Nothing is. But, like all other worthwhile ideas, it helps. And it can lead to something else.

For instance, all those simple instructions which it does

not occur to them to disobey. Keep building on that. The more they fall in with what you want in these small things, the greater the grip you are gaining. You are getting through to the subconscious. Exploit it.

Or again, one thing can lead to another. Say you suddenly need a red biro, and you don't have one with you. What do you do? You say, 'Anyone got a red biro? I have these late books to mark.'

Rest assured, somebody will. And only too willing to offer it. It is a rare class that can not muster a red biro between them, and an extremely bolshy class that, to a man, refuses to oblige.

Once again, it's tiny, but it provides an infinitesimal dollop of class glue. And the great joy is that you can do it again. And they will respond again. Show them your little pile of late exercise books, and out will flash the red biros.

What starts as a favour turns into a joke, evolves into a habit, matures into a tradition, and finally emerges as a ritual. They adore rituals. Let them see a small clutch of late exercise books under your arm, and at once you are knee-deep in red biros. Curiously, they don't say, 'Why the hell don't you go out and buy a red biro, sir?' No. It would spoil the ritual.

What have you done? You have got them responding to one of your wishes before you have even asked them. Getting through to the subconscious again. Well done.

A final word on repetition. The idea has cropped up several times in this piece. Using good ideas over and over again. Developing further examples is only repetition in disguise. If you haven't already worked out the value of it, you most certainly will – if you want to carry on being a teacher, that is.

Never be afraid to repeat. Comedians repeat their best jokes – we still laugh at them. (Alas, they still repeat some of their worst ones.) I have never heard of any authority on education who warns against the dire dangers of repetition. What are the parts of our primary education that we remember the longest? Our tables. Think of how many times we recited them. One totalitarian regime after another has relied on repetition in its propaganda. Think of the number of advertising jingles we can repeat as easy as pie – and we were not even listening. Try telling a child his favourite bedtime story; Heaven help you if you get one of the details wrong.

A young Chemistry teacher said in the common room one day, 'I have got right through the exam syllabus for the year, and it's only March. What do I do?'

Said his head of department, without even taking his eyes off the crossword, 'Go through it all again; they won't mind.'

A worldly voice muttered, 'They won't even know.'

Glib, yes. There is more to it than being small and simple and saying it lots of times. It helps if you're polite too.

2 Good manners

ONE OR TWO OBSERVATIONS to begin with.

Manners vary. It is well known that what may be acceptable in one society or one set of circumstances may give offence in others. A retired colonial administrator told the tale of his fresh arrival in the (then) Gilbert and Ellice Islands in the South Pacific, and being offered a drink by a young girl on one of his first rounds of inspection. He took a casual swig, said 'Thank you', and handed the coconut back. The little girl was clearly upset. When he asked why, she explained that she had no knowledge of whether he had enjoyed it or not, because he had not given evidence of it. When he asked her what she meant, she demonstrated by letting rip with a cavernous burp which shook her tiny body from stem to stern.

These variations may be difficult to predict or understand, and can lead to anything from annoyance and embarrassment to ground-rolling hysterics. What I am concerned with here is not the anthropological side of it all, but what you might call the moral core of it.

Put more simply, a teacher should take care that he says and does nothing which may upset the sensibilities of his pupils. Even more simply, he should pay attention to the 'Please' and 'Thank you' dimensions of good manners. Though, with the increasing variations of race, religion, and culture in our schools, it might pay him to become just a little aware of the 'big burp' feature of it too.

Incidentally, while we are still on the subject of the big burp, it is arguable that the little girl herself was guilty of poor manners, because she pointed out to a guest that he had committed a social error of which he was ignorant, and he might have become embarrassed. However, as she was only seven years old in the story, and the situation was making demands upon her discretion which were beyond her years, one can perhaps forgive her; after all, she had tried to be hospitable.

Aside from the philosophy and the anecdote, I don't think any reasonable person would argue that good manners have no place in teaching, though a little explanation and a few examples might help to get the point across.

There is always a danger too that a teacher who tries hard to be polite will be a sitting duck for the tike and scallywag brigade, to say nothing of those with more than a nodding acquaintance with delinquency, disruption, and crime. But that is unavoidable in a world full of all those sorts who famously make it. It is no argument for giving up good manners that some people have bad ones, or none. A solution has to be found, and we are always looking.

However, time for some brass tacks.

It is a curious thing that a lot of parents will not lose much sleep over the fact their son or daughter has been involved a spot of petty larceny or a dust-up in the playground or some hot-cheeked shenanigans behind the bike sheds, but very few take pride in their offspring being known as bad-mannered.

Good manners, then, are generally valued, so you, as a teacher, are on to a good thing if you encourage them, and even more so if you practise them.

It is true that, as a teacher, you are part of a hierarchical organisation. By virtue of your education, your diploma, and your status in that organisation, you are entitled to a measure of respect. So yes, you can demand it if you like, and with some justification. But it is better to earn it. That way, it is given more freely, and it is genuine. It is always better to have the genuine article.

One of the ways to earn it is to be polite. 'Please', 'thank you', 'would you be kind enough', 'I'd be grateful if', and all the rest are easy to say, cost nothing, and go a mighty long way – regardless of the age or status of the person to whom they are addressed.

Offer politeness; you usually get it back.

I had a Latin teacher who could be irascible at times, if we were dilatory about memorising our irregular verbs. But he still accorded us dignity. He always addressed us as 'gentlemen'. Treated us as if we were undergraduates. We weren't of course, but the point was that he was giving us the credit for being able to *behave* as undergraduates. So, even in our inadequate way, we tried to live up to it. What annoyed him was not our immaturity; it was our laziness with Latin verbs.

If you're polite, especially with those further down the scale than you, it's part of showing that you understand their position. It may be lowlier than yours, but just as deserving of respect. People like to be understood.

Similarly with punctuality. Pupils have a right to expect a full lesson, not one cut short because you don't look at your watch often enough.

There is another angle to this – the mathematical one. If you are ten minutes late for a forty-minute lesson, do the sums. That's 25% of their teaching time. Make a habit of that, and, in a two-period-a-week subject, over the course of an academic year of 35 weeks, you are short-changing them to the tune of nearly 12 hours. In a five-period-a-week subject like English or Maths, you are letting them down to the tune of just over 29 hours. Just think of all the agonising that has been going on during the last two years or so, about how much schooling our children are said to be losing because of Covid, to say nothing of the dreadful mental anguish concomitally involved. At the very least, it makes you think.

So is the regularly late teacher causing widespread decline in pupils' mental health? I wouldn't know, but, as I said, it does offer another reason for being on time, besides pure good manners.

It's no good explaining either, when you arrive in a gale of disarray and apology. You make it worse when you mop your brow and gasp excuses to explain why. You wouldn't make excuses if you didn't think you were in the wrong. No teacher is so brass-necked or thick-skinned that he turns up a quarter of an hour late and says, 'Hard luck; I just didn't feel like hurrying today.' No. You make excuses.

The more excuses you make, the less currency they have. What starts as a surprise becomes a nuisance, then a joke, a bore, finally a sort of cross. You wouldn't tolerate it if a pupil was regularly late for a lesson; you would do something about it. There is not much a class can do with a teacher who can't or won't turn up on time. They can't put him in detention. The most they can do is dislike him. But think of the effect on their attitude and morale. If you want to eat away at a class's respect for you, it's an infallible way to do it. And it's only a type of bad manners, so eminently remediable.

Is that it then? Say please and turn up on time? As I have said before (and will no doubt say again), there is a little more to it than that.

Such as? Well, for instance, what do you look like? People can be very touchy about this. A lot can, and no doubt will, be said about an adult's freedom of choice, the tyranny of over-formality, the need to keep up with current fashion, the very natural urge *not* to look like a schoolteacher. We can easily wander into cliché country too, with talk of chalk dust, shiny suits, handbags, and 'sensible' shoes. I suggest that most of this is pretty feeble.

Nobody wants you to dress 'like a teacher' – if such a state is possible. What are you saying then? Not much really, beyond a few tentative suggestions and a point or two which you may have overlooked.

In no particular order, you are not on a desert island. (If you were, chances are you wouldn't be wearing very much at all.) In teaching, there are people all around you, and the majority of them are young. The young need guidance, moderation, example, and sheer reasonability. For all their capacity for sedition, the young can be very conservative; they actually like habit, predictability, ordinariness, and reliability. They may moan about it sometimes, even laugh at it, but, on balance, they would like a modest percentage of that ordinariness and formality to be there, and available.

I put it to the court that they would not find it comfortable if their teachers dressed like something straight off the catwalk or fresh out of Savile Row. It would take their minds off learning, and the most rebellious of them, if pushed back to the wall, would admit that that is what they expect their teachers to do – teach, not dress up.

Not dress down either. They would not like their

teachers to look like something the cat brought in. Heaven knows, there's plenty of room for choice in between.

Something suitable – isn't that you aim for? You are teaching. You wouldn't expect a navvy to turn up at the roadworks in a bow tie and plus fours. Well, if you are young and female, is it a good idea to go in front of a class of fifteen-year-old boys in a mini-skirt, platform heels, and see-through blouse? No matter how high-powered you are, they won't be thinking much about quadratic equations. Freedom here is not wrong; it is just stupid. Not only should you aim to respect their sensibilities; you should avoid inflaming them too. All part of good manners – aiming in the end to produce peace, comfort and an atmosphere conducive to learning. It is the very lack of sensation you want; so that they hardly know that some education is going on. Do nothing to disturb it. It's the unobtrusiveness that you are after. A novelist wants you to read his story, not his words. Similarly, you should want them to get the lesson, not the teacher.

Look at it the reverse way: could you, offhand, think of any good results that would come about if you looked untidy, unwholesome, or provocative? And not just with clothes; with hair, makeup, fingernails, neckline, stains, holes, dangling buttons, anything.

With other things too, which are so observable to pupils. You may not have much time to sit and observe twenty-five or thirty pupils – individually – in a forty-minute period, but they have a pretty fair opportunity in that forty minutes to observe you. Do you lean against things? Do you lollop about? Do you lounge when you sit down? Do you sprawl? Are you weighed down with too many bags, cases, and papers? Can you find things when you want them? Like that elusive red biro?

Do you look disorganised? Are you taken by surprise too often? Constantly caught out. Do you fluster easily?

All these complaints are curable. You won't make things perfect, but you can make them better.

As with boy scouts – or so they tell us – being prepared is half the battle. Yet, even if you manage that, and the lesson is going like clockwork, it is no excuse for relaxing. The classroom is a formal situation; it is not a sitting room or a bar lounge. It remains a formal situation despite whatever success you achieve.

At the risk of preaching (again), this 'general smartness' approach, conveying the sense of 'with-it-ness', helps to get across the idea that you regard the lesson as important enough for you to take trouble, both with your class and with yourself. It shows that you are aware of the impression you are making. It all helps to make them feel that you think they are worth it.

Something else which makes them feel they are 'worth it' is the simple business of listening. This is so obvious, isn't it? We are all supposed to listen – to what people say to us. Not just in the classroom; listening well is good manners anywhere. It is especially important in teaching (as in being a priest, or a nurse, or a doctor).

Children may get fed up with being seen and not heard, but they can live with that now and again if they have to. But they all want to be noticed. One can tolerate being disagreed with, argued with, shouted at, sworn at, and all the rest. But the worst of all is to be ignored.

In a class, every pupil has a right to be heard. Better still, listened to. That is what you are there for. If you don't, that's bad manners. It doesn't matter if they are not talking brilliant common sense. Very few of us do most of the time.

In a routine question-and-answer session, not only keep your ears open; keep your antennae out. Not only for the answers you are expecting, but for the ones you are not expecting. Even if they are wrong. They can strike a spark even if they don't hit the nail smack on the head.

Give praise for thinking, for imagination, for near misses. It gives them confidence. Remember, every time they open their mouths to answer one of your questions, not only are you listening; twenty-five or thirty other people are listening as well, and they can be much more cruel than you – we hope. If you don't give them credit for trying, you are in danger of suggesting that they don't have anything to offer that's worth listening to. Before long, they may not feel like bothering again (would you?), and you are left with only the little swots thrusting their hands up.

There's another problem, even if they know the answer, and even if they know they're right: pupils are all different.

Now there's a profound statement. What wisdom! What perception!

But such a basic truth is easily overlooked or forgotten. Especially if a teacher has given a particular lesson several times; if he's tired (a very familiar condition); if he's under any kind of pressure, which means that he has to devote valuable wits to some problem or other – wits he should be devoting to the class in front of him. It is so easy to switch on the automatic pilot – all the more tempting the more experienced a teacher is. Perhaps one of the advantages the beginner has over the veteran is that he doesn't have an automatic pilot to switch on. Well, not yet. He has to concentrate, if he knows what's good for him.

Brass tacks time again. Some pupils are louder than others; some are more talkative than others; some pupils simply have more to say than others, for good or ill. That does not mean that they are naughty, or disruptive, or anti-education (though a few obviously will be). It simply means that they are different. It is just their way.

At the other end of the scale are the quiet ones. They don't like drawing attention to themselves. If any limelight shows up, they will go a long way round to avoid it. That does not make them mice, or ignoramuses, or self-effacing nobodies. It is just their way too.

They can be just as intelligent, just as attentive (often more so, certainly more than you might think, because you don't notice), just as likely to know the right answer. They can mop it up just the same as any of the loud ones; look at what they write in their summer exam. You find that it has all gone in, and you never realised.

These are the ones whom it is so easy to overlook; there is no noise coming from them. It is very easy to allow your attention to be drawn to where the noise *is* coming from. It is not a question of goodness or naughtiness. With some children you always know they are there; with others you don't. I repeat, it is just their way. Variations like this can occur in families as well as in classes. Oddly, individual pupils can vary as well between class and family. Many a time a teacher will hear at a parents' evening, 'That's odd; she doesn't behave like that at home.'

Children – pupils, young people, whatever you like – are complicated.

It is up to the teacher to be aware of this truth all the

time. Of course, he can't carry around with him a Pupil Attention Meter to monitor how much attention he gives to each one, but he should, at the least, be aware that the problem exists.

The talkative pupil knows he will get his share of Sir's attention, because he's making a noise; the quiet one can not be so sure. But – but – if a girl feels that she is getting a fair crack of the whip from a teacher, the teacher will draw loyalty from her – often more than average, because that girl is so grateful.

Perhaps equally important, you, the teacher, will have earned that loyalty. And you didn't do it by blazing charisma, or top-heavy brain power, or fancy gimmicks; you did it by simple kindness and fairness. The man up the road can do that. So can you.

If you are punctual, polite, and presentable, you are trying, and visibly trying, to make a favourable impression, and they are hard nuts indeed if they do not respond just a little. Being a good listener; being attentive. Making sure that every pupil in the lesson is getting a fair share of your best.

As with all other advice on teaching, nothing is the last word, nothing is the magic formula; nothing is the 'Open Sesame!' to glittering success. But it all helps. It all can be built on. How can you do the building?

3 Good practices

I HAVE NO PROFESSIONAL knowledge of psychology, so it will not carry much weight when I say that one of the hallmarks of intelligence is clarity – clarity of thought and clarity of expression; it is just one man's opinion.

But I do know something about teaching, so I dare to hope that it may carry a little more weight when I say that clarity is one of the hallmarks of good teaching. When you set out to teach a class something, your intention is to make it clear, so that they have a better chance of understanding it. If, by the end of the topic, or the course, or the year, they haven't got it, something is not quite right. Hardly an educational triumph for you, is it?

Notice I did not say 'liking it'; I said 'understanding it'. The two are not necessarily the same. You can be turned on by the whole idea, say, of cosmic navigation – even find it thrilling – but you know that you will never master it. Similarly, a good teacher will give you mastery over Latin verbs, but when the course is over and you have passed with distinction, you may never open a Latin grammar again for the rest of your life.

There are other factors too – the pupil's IQ, the amount of time he is allocated to do the learning, the general morale of the class, the level of discipline in the school, and no doubt many more. But this book is concerned with the teacher's point of view, and from the teacher's point of view, you further the cause by being as clear as you can.

Ah, yes, reducing it to basics, boiling it all right down. No. I said '*making it clear*', not making it simple. Certainly not necessarily easy. Going back to my Latin teacher again, Bunter (that was his nickname – Bunter – long story) never went out of his way to disguise the problem. Latin was difficult; he made no bones about it. (Greek was worse.) He never made excuses for his subject. But he did claim – and he was deeply sincere about this – that, if you could do Latin and Greek, you could tackle anything. He was absolutely sure that the study of 'Classics' was the finest training for the human mind yet devised by the brain of man.

That did not mean that he looked down on other subjects. On the contrary. He had more knowledge of subjects outside his own than any other teacher I have ever met – before or since. We respected, and envied, both his knowledge and his conviction. How splendid it was to be so confident in what you were doing.

Perhaps I have laboured this point, and I apologise. But I happen to think you can't over-emphasise it.

So I shall repeat it. *Be clear.*

Look at your teaching notes. The words and sentences. The *organisation* of them. Don't look at them as the author. Of course they're easy; you wrote them, and you know exactly what you mean. You know them inside out.

Your pupils don't. It's all new to them. They don't make the leaps of almost instinctive understanding based on long knowledge and experience because they haven't got much. You, the teacher, are making these leaps all the time without thinking. It is easy to forget that you once found it difficult.

It requires another leap too – this time of the imagination – to be able to see this material with the eyes of a young person coming to it for the first time.

The more you examine your notes, your script – your 'homework', if you like – in a back-handed sort of way, you get better at it yourself. Your grip gets more sure. Cut out surplus padding here; change a section there; add a vital factor to the equation somewhere else; switch items in the batting order of points so that the argument becomes more logical – the more care you take in fashioning your material, the better the article you produce. You find yourself understanding it better than you did before you began struggling to bring it into order.

Hence the wry little comment, well understood in the profession, that if you want to learn a subject, teach it.

Whatever you do, it must be in the cause of seeing that they 'get it', if not straight off the bat, then after several innings. We are back to the mantra of repetition. You have to make sure. At every stage. If they miss one, it gets harder to keep up. If the process degenerates into deepening fog and regular failure, then anybody, never mind a disillusioned pupil, would feel like giving up.

In an attempt to bypass such a situation, in the effort of getting your message across, don't be tempted to pare it down. Making it clear does not mean making it easy. That way lies trouble. The more they get the impression that you have made it all easy, the less they have respect for it. If they think it's a doddle, they're on the high road to slapdashery. No subject ('academic' or otherwise) is intrinsically easy, not if it is taught properly.

Yes, every subject may have its easy bits, and success in getting that across is no great achievement. But if you can tackle the difficult bits, and make them appreciate just how difficult they are, and still get it across, then you are a good teacher. If you can get them to enjoy it as well, then you are one hell of a good teacher.

While all that is going on, there will be countless

decisions you will have to take, some important ones, many lesser ones, right down to scores of others which verge on the trivial. Whatever they are, they will affect a classful of young people, all of whom have an acute sense of justice. Now and then, this may be a little overblown, but the protest, when it comes, can often reflect a grievance keenly felt at the time. It can be very quick too, almost reflex.

You may not always sympathise, but you have to be aware of the strength of feeling involved, and handle it with the degree of sensitivity required.

In as few words as possible: 'Be fair.'

I do not refer to differences between individual pupils. For them you may need a whole new batch of Solomonic skills, beyond the brief of this chapter. No. I mean the situations which arise between pupil and teacher.

We know that you are trying manfully, all the time, to be the perfect paragon of the ideal president, the just arbiter, and the merciful judge. But there will be times when, with the best will in the world, you will give offence.

Very often, of course, you won't know you've committed it, so there is nothing to be done. But if and when somebody tells you, then something *has* to be done.

If you can convince the pupil that no offence in fact was either committed or intended, then your own conscience is clear. If the pupil continues to harbour a grudge, that is his problem, and there is nothing to be done about that either.

If harm was done, but you didn't know you were offending at the time, then you have a case. But you still have no guarantee that the chip will not settle on the shoulder; you will have to live with the surly looks for a while.

On rarer occasions, you may know that you were going to upset somebody with your decision, but circumstances were such that you had no alternative to doing what you did, even knowing that it would appear unfair. This, more than any other 'offence', has to be explained – quickly, privately, thoroughly, and truthfully.

If the chip remains embedded in the shoulder, you will have to live with it. You will have done your best. Don't beat your breast; don't wear sackcloth and ashes. Just carry on business as usual. You can't orient the whole class round one pupil, however hard done by he may feel.

All you can do is hope that he will come round with time, and with observing from day-to-day contact thereafter that you are not a monster of arbitrary cruelty. But nothing is certain. You can't win them all. You can try, but there is no guarantee that you will succeed. One tactic which stands a chance is to give the pupil the benefit of the doubt. To hope that he will understand.

You also try sticking to your guns In other words, not allowing yourself to be a soft touch, You don't always have to use vinegar; honey can work too.

Say a pupil comes up to you, bursting with courtesy and charm, and asks silkily whether you could possibly change the day on which you have sentenced him to an after-school detention, because he already had a long-standing and much-looked-forward-to event scheduled for that day and that time. (The institution of detention may be slipping out of date, but the point is just as valid.) He would be only too happy to do the detention on any other day you cared to name.

Now courtesy and charm, as that pupil well knows, can go a long way, so try switching the same tactic on him:

'Yes, I hear you, John, and I quite understand. And thank you for your politeness. I appreciate the urgency of your engagement. But I have to point out to you that a detention is a punishment for something you have done wrong, and you graciously admit that you committed the offence.

'Now the whole point of a punishment is that it should be inconvenient. If I bend the arrangements to fit in with your plans, I am turning the system on its head. The detention virtually ceases to be a punishment. I'm very sorry, but I have a responsibility to maintain the force of the system. I have no choice.'

A glittering smile from yourself may help to consummate the lightweight charm offensive. If that pupil has half a sense of humour, he should get the point. If he doesn't, well, you have tried. You have listened, you have weighed his request, and you have given a decision as charming as his request.

You have been reasonable, and you have given him a glance into how the system works. And, thank God, your discipline (if not your popularity ratio) is still intact.

Everyone values reasonability. It is up to a teacher to show that he too values it, that he practises it, and that he tries to develop respect for it in his pupils.

They are not born with it. The new-born baby is the ultimate merciless survivor; he yells for attention until he gets it, and he doesn't say thank you. He only yells again when he wants something else. (He doesn't have much choice, poor little scrap, does he?) He is not interested in what anybody else wants; he doesn't even know. His entire world is fifteen inches of cradle or pram walls. It is somewhat limiting.

As he grows, a child has a million things to learn. One of the hardest is to cotton on to the idea that other people have needs and desires that are just as valid as his own. As he learns from parents, brothers and sisters, play group, nursery, and school, he begins to get a glimmering of what being reasonable means.

It begins to sink in that reasonableness is something worth having. He grows enough self-knowledge to be aware that he doesn't always show it himself – well, not enough. But, from a philosophical point of view, he understands the value of it.

If all goes well, he will see it in his mother and father. That is where you come in; he needs to be able to see it in his teachers. He may not be able to define what 'being reasonable' is, but he learns to know it when he sees it. And he also learns to be aware when it's not there.

As with so many ideas to do with education, it is a brave expert who attempts a definition of it. (No wonder the poor pupil can't do it.) But we all know that it is a vital ingredient in the character of all adults who have to deal with children (with everybody). It may be a somewhat woolly subject, but it would be silly and pointless to try and argue it away. You might as well try to give a definition of goodness, or attempt an argument either to justify it or to nullify its value.

Let's get away from the philosophy for a moment, and consider some personal practicalities. What do you do about yourself during a lesson? Your sheer physical presence? You are a key element in the impact of the lesson. You are large (don't forget they are sitting down most of the time), you are the one with initiative. You are the one who decides what to do, how to get the lesson over. You are the most interesting thing in the room for the next thirty or forty minutes. How do you use yourself?

For instance, are you a stander or a wanderer? As a corollary to that, do you do it from a desk, or from your own two feet? Always bear in mind, by the way, the advantage of greater height. From the dawn of ancient warfare, cavalry have always looked more impressive than infantry; they are right up high.

Again, do you prefer to operate by remote control? Or, like medieval kings, do you feel that you need to be everywhere? This may be a simple matter of sheer personal comfort. Does lack of motion assist concentration? Or do you think best when you're moving? Think of all those great statesmen and tycoons who can't dictate letters unless they're pacing up and down. Which would you rather be? A firm focus, or a moving target?

There is little point in pontificating on this. I suggest there is no right and wrong; it would depend on circumstances, individual personalities, the nature of the work in hand, the size of the class, the size of the room – a host of things. Nor do you have to plump for one strategy or the other, and then stick to it through thick and thin.

I think perhaps the only sensible thing to do is to point out that the topic is there; that it merits your consideration; and that it is up to you to evolve a strategy, a method, an approach, which suits you, suits them, and suits the lesson – at the time.

If you want a theme, a motif, a 'spirit', whatever you like, I would suggest that you go for comfort. Everybody likes comfort. If nothing else, comfortable classes are less likely to misbehave; it's too much trouble. Upsets things.

Nobody likes moving from something comfortable to something uncomfortable.

Finally, a very effective method – possibly the best of all – for preventing the very idea of disturbance even entering their heads – is having something to do. (Yet another revelation of blinding obviousness.) One of the best generators of mayhem is inactivity, lack of lesson purpose, and, ultimately, boredom. Think of that powerhouse of submerged energy and burgeoning biology surging away, stuck for hours at unyielding desks that get smaller every year. Something needs to be happening all the time.

In a word – well, two – be busy.

However many minutes the lesson may last for, fill them. Don't take a long time to get going. And don't be tempted to knock off early.

I had another Latin teacher who was gruff, crusty, and not over-endowed with patience, but we knew that, if the lesson was scheduled to run for forty minutes, that meant forty minutes of undiluted Latin. We knew where we were. We knew exactly what we were going to get. He was reliable. Pupils do so value reliability.

We were too young to appreciate what the word 'professional' meant – not fully. Looking back, though, I think what we valued about him was his professionalism. Like Frank Sinatra and his songs (see Chapter One).

Don't relax. If you get a good class and they mop up the work like mad, have more work ready. Prepare more work than you think you are going to need. Never run out. If you do, it will show; you have been caught out. A hole will begin to appear in the dyke. Get it filled – quickly. Think of something. Like the Army: make 'em dig holes and fill 'em in again.

Possibly the best bit of encouragement I had during my first year's teaching was a remark dropped by my first headmaster. He was a regular visitor for one admin. reason or another; he didn't have a secretary (he was keeping an eye on me too, I expect). One day, after looking round the room, he leaned towards me conspiratorially and whispered, 'Y'know, one thing I like – whenever I come in here, they're doing something.'

I treasured that.

A busy class is not silent. It is not disturbed either. Anything but. It gives off so many soft sounds: tiny tics as pens are put down, the little clack of a ruler, rustles and shuffles, scrapes of chairs, a cupboard being opened; a zip on a pencil case. Even more subtle: it's an air, an atmosphere, an *ambiance*. If you are in the trade, it's unmistakable. It's a lovely noise.

So, if you have been paying attention, I have been offering five pieces of portentous advice: Be clear; be fair; be reasonable; be still (at least comfortable), and be busy.

All right. You follow those hints. Well done. Are you on your way?

Not necessarily; something will come up.

4 Breaking the flow

THE CLOSER YOU ARE to the start of your teaching career, the less experience you have, so the more likely you are to be caught off balance by surprises. Obviously, the more experience you gain, the sum total of things that happen doesn't contain so many surprises, because you've seen it before.

Nevertheless, always keep one of your wits in reserve. However much you know, or have seen, you must be prepared for the really outrageous happening, the maverick impossibility, the million-to-one coincidence of events which could test you to your limits, however far along the road to retirement you are. You can't guarantee that you will cope with cavalier brilliance, swashbuckling *panache*, or weary disdain. If God is kind, you will come through with your nerves-ends, and your reputation, unshredded.

Perhaps the best you can hope for, realistically, is that your after-dinner repertoire is going to be enhanced by a good story, even if it is at your expense.

All this, I suppose, amounts to little more than a word of warning that you should not ever reach the stage where you fancy that you know it all. Incidentally, never be bemused into uncritical admiration of the teacher who *seems* to know it all. Common sense should tell you that he probably doesn't. If he *behaves* as if he knows it all, he most certainly doesn't.

Be that as it may, let us consider practicalities. However well you are prepared, or however hard you work, things will happen, things will come up, things will 'gang a-gley', and possibly quite 'aft'.

Such as?

Ah, there, Watson, you take us into deep waters. I can not tell you what the unexpected will be, because then it wouldn't be unexpected, and it would be much easier to deal with. All I can do is mention just a few *types* of circumstance, and suggest a few *types* of reaction which may help you to deal with the situation.

For instance, take the question of authority. Your authority. Your authority in the classroom. What is the biggest worry for an actor? Is it forgetting his lines? Is it the make-up melting and running? The props not working? No. It's: will the audience like him? What is the biggest worry for a teacher? Is it the quality of his degree? How well he has mastered his material? No. It's: will he be able to keep order?

Order, order, order. That is the top priority. Any other problem will have to take second place. There's one of you and up to thirty (or more) of them. However hard you work to maintain harmony, peace, and good relations, something is bound to come up which has the potential to threaten that happy state of affairs.

There will be a problem, a disagreement, a clash, a stalemate. How many odds are stacked against you? You know, and they know, that the verdict, the decision, will lie with you; that's what you're there for. You have the authority, and, in principle, they do not challenge it. In principle.

But pupils do not always think first of principles; they think of more immediate issues, the nuts and bolts of the dispute. There is the solution staring the teacher in the face. What do you do? Do you take shelter behind the ramparts of 'Order'? Knowing that the authorities will back you? Will the members of the class think as highly of authority as you do? Is it expecting them to have older heads on their shoulders than they actually do?

It is here that you must ponder hard, and give credit to principles beside the sacred one of 'Order'. Your brain tells you that order is not the be-all and end-all. You must also learn to respect common sense, sheer logic, natural justice, the truth, even Fate. You must be ready to give way if that's how the cards lie.

It's all right; your rule will not shiver and collapse. Not if you give way with grace. Give them credit for understanding things like that. They often do. They will appreciate it too. They can, now and again, let you down, but the potential dividend is worth the risk.

As I said in the previous chapter, there will be times too when you will give offence. You didn't mean to. But you have. It may be that you have offended a single pupil. Worse, you have offended him in front of other people. Worse still (I know; I have done it) you have upset a whole class.

If you do that, and in any other circumstances in which an apology is clearly needed, you must give it. *And you must mean it.* As one human being to another. They will often value apologies above compliments; they cost more.

Another surprise which you can almost guarantee will happen sooner or later is the phenomenon of the joke.

Heaven forbid, I don't mean the teacher opening the proceedings with: 'A funny thing happened to me on the way to school this morning.' It is not your function to be an entertainer. Young pupils can be more critical of a teacher usurping the role of stand-up comedian than the toughest of first houses in a Glasgow variety theatre on a

Monday night. If you are not good at telling jokes, don't tell 'em. Even if you are, don't. Tempting. But don't. It can so easily go wrong. Yet another surprise. And it's the very devil to recover from. Worse still, it's your own fault.

Tiny, throwaway illustrative anecdotes, maybe, but not jokes.

An even greater chasm that can gape at the teacher's feet is the Russian roulette of exchanging witticisms with a pupil. As sure as eggs, you will end up with one of them on your face. Never, never, take on the class wag.

No. What I am talking about is the joke played on you as the teacher. I am simply saying that it helps if you can see it. By virtue of the fact that it is a joke, it is by definition a surprise, so you will need that spare wit I spoke about.

Now, there are good jokes and nasty jokes. One can usually tell the difference. Let us hope that you are never the butt or the victim of the latter. If you are, it is not your fault, and you have no need to reproach yourself. And if you do not have the stripes on your sleeve to enable you to deal with it, it is no weakness to call in somebody who does.

Most jokes, though, are free from spite, and it is a rather touchy teacher who does not share in them. If he is that touchy, the chances are that the class will not take the trouble to play a joke on him; there will be no entertainment in it. A joke from a class is often a sign of intimacy and good relations, so it can be comforting.

At other times, a laugh can be generated from the oddest of happenings – an outrageously wrong answer, a couple of sentences at cross purposes, a dramatic breakage with tsunami fall-out, a sudden entrance at a most inopportune moment, and so on. Whatever it is, treasure it; there is no better lubrication for a lesson than a good, shared, healthy laugh.

Talking of unexpected entrances, far more frequent than the loud irruption, the dramatic arrival, is the *undramatic* arrival. The routine visit, the necessary call, the daily round. They are teeth-grindingly ordinary, but they can drive you to near-murderous fury.

Consider. You have prepared at length, worked with mole-like devotion and intensity to set the stage for one of your show-piece expositions, a masterstroke of debate, a climax of imminent high drama. It is going well; the plans are all falling into place; you've got them; they are in the palm of your hand; they are actually listening. Not just politely tolerating you; actually listening. You can hear them listening. You come to the Great Moment…

Somebody comes in with a message about appointments for the school dentist. Worse, two or three of them have to get up and leave. Books away, desks shutting, standing up, footsteps, a snicker or two about drills, everyone watching the door shutting.

It's all gone. Humpty-Dumpty has fallen off the wall. How much time do you have left to put him together again?

That is for you to judge. It is very difficult to mend broken 'Moments'. That very instant can become one of the jokes you need to see the point of. Because they will probably laugh – heartless beasts. You will probably have to wait a day or two and start all over again. But my word, it does test the patience.

Incidentally, this is yet another justification for the advice about preparing more work than you expect to need, because this is one of the times when you are going to need it. The lesson – your *pièce de résistance* – is in tatters.

Time to show those wits I have spoken about, your professionalism, your foresight, your *sang froid*, your simple gumption, even your character if you like. Instead of it being a minor disaster, it could, possibly, be made into an opportunity. Now that really is smart teaching.

You will have used that spare wit – the strategic reserve. Use it as well to keep a weather eye open (or a weather ear) for any show of spark by pupils. I don't mean 'wit', humour, smart-alecry. I mean 'wits' – a shrewd remark, a snappy summary, a neat phrase, that just came out. He or she hadn't been labouring on it for weeks, like Oscar Wilde with his ad-libs; I mean something that just, as I said, came out. It came out because the pupil had been paying attention, had shown interest, had caught the drift, and was ready to make a contribution that was both helpful and relevant, sometimes even original.

The point is that it was unexpected. All I am suggesting is that the teacher keeps an antenna at the ready to catch it.

This story is not strictly relevant from a factual point of view, but it illustrates the principle of the capacity of the subordinate to surprise his superior with an action that can be both immediate and effective.

There was an admiral who set great store by keeping his junior officers on their toes, by means of unpredictable actions which made sudden and unexpected demands on their capacity for initiative.

He was carrying out an inspection on a warship one day, and a lively young midshipman was showing him round one of the upper decks. They were standing by the rail, when, without any warning, the old sea-dog whipped off his cap, flung it on the deck at the midshipman's feet and barked, 'That's an unexploded bomb. What are you doing to do about it?'

Without a moment's hesitation, the boy kicked it into the water.

That's all I wanted to say: underlings can surprise you. Be ready to give credit for it.

I was taking a sixth form for an 'A' Level History lesson, and the topic under discussion was the medieval Catholic Church. I was explaining the regular practice they employed of endowing anything connected with the hierarchy of saints with great reverence. Particularly physical parts of them. Long after they were dead. It was common practice for the Faithful to make long journeys simply to pray at the shrine of a saint, or part of a saint. It was believed that by so doing they could glean great Heavenly grace, and thereby cut short the length of time they would have to spend in Purgatory, where their sins were cleansed prior to joining Jesus and Mary in Paradise. A lot of money changed hands too when the pilgrims made grateful offerings at the church or shrine where the saint's bones, or bone, rested.

Human nature being what it is, a lot of money was raised from the credulous Faithful by setting up holy relics to be worshipped which were neither holy nor relics. It was a scandal which lasted for centuries. The class duly took in all this.

A few days later, like all teachers, I began a revision session, and said we were going to return to the business of holy relics.

One boy nodded knowledgeably. 'Ah, yes,' he said.

'The bones scam.'

I had never heard that phrase before, and I don't know how he got hold of it, or whether he had coined it. But even if it was not original, it fits my point. Whether I, as an 'A' Level History teacher, should have known it is irrelevant. He had said something apposite, and I had been sharp-witted enough to spot it. I realised that it hit a very useful nail smack on the head. It had the correct combination of neatness, understanding, informality, and modernity that would go down easily with a class of seventeen-year-olds. Because of his age, and mine, he was more likely to have used it than I was. But I could see that, for all its glibness, it would work. I used it several times in other lessons with other classes.

We come now to the surprise which is not a surprise.

We are back to planning again. It is true that all teachers have to deal with surprises and interruptions, but one can hope that, with experience, he – or she (let's say 'she' for a change) will get better at dealing with them. She will *have* to get better; the number of them is not likely to diminish: those dental appointments, somebody fainting, a broken window (whether by inside or outside agency), a visit by a governor, another one by an inspector, a third by an increasingly regular phenomenon, an adviser.

If you went back far enough, you could add morning milk, the sacred ritual of the register, the distribution of text-books, canvassing for an audience for a forthcoming school revue, advertising a projected foreign trip, a power cut. Go back further, and you could mention an air raid, a bomb, or a V-2 rocket. (Try putting the lesson together after that).

Time, technology, educational philosophy, and no

doubt many others will continue to make inroads. I'm sure I have only scratched the surface. Any teacher could add his own two penn'orth. It almost makes you wonder how anybody got, or gets, any teaching done at all.

So watch out.

Back to the surprise that is not a surprise. Why? Because you set it up yourself.

This is something you will get better at as you go along. Part of the advanced course, as you might say.

As you go along, and you keep looking and listening – to colleagues and pupils, parents and 'experts', your instincts and common sense – you gain comfort from the fact that you are learning something, but you also have to deal with the dismaying realisation that there is so much more waiting to be learnt.

Say you find that you are teaching the same lesson several times. That is inevitable: the syllabuses don't change every year (though sometimes you wonder, when you hear those 'experts', planners, and philosophers in full flow); you may have more than one class in that particular year; you are notching up several years of service at the same school.

This can have two effects. As I have said elsewhere, you are finding the work more and more undemanding, because it's becoming routine; you are forgetting that you once found it difficult; you are overlooking those leaps of learning which you perform effortlessly, and which they find hard. So in a sense you could get a little worse.

But – fortunately – you could also get better. You think of neater ways to present something; you tumble to an improved technique; you smarten up your teaching notes, which are getting a little frayed at the edges. You learn to foresee more snags and problems. You can hold their hand to guide them round the holes and the puddles on the path.

That's where you have the edge on them. You are getting better with each stab at it. (Well, we hope so.) They have only one bite. This is where you can maybe spring a few little surprises which illustrate something or other. You can appear to break the rules, make it look as if you've gone wrong, and 'Presto!' – you solve the problem at a stroke. A little trick of the trade. But don't be tempted to do it too often.

You know what's coming; they don't. Anything which puts you ahead in the game is worth considering. You are learning that teaching is not only an art; it is a craft.

And even this knack has to be managed. You learn to bring off all these little coups. Well done. But ration it. As with everything else, the watchword is moderation. Don't let them conclude that your briefcase contains nothing but a bag of tricks. The ballast, the weight of knowledge, the hard graft, should always be there. If you are seduced by the success of those little tricks, they will rumble you. Think of that Latin teacher and his forty minutes of solid Latin. When all is said and done, you can't beat work.

I have strayed somewhat from the title towards the end of this chapter, so perhaps it is apt to go back and offer a short summary. I am concerned with the things that can upset, or at least interfere with, the flow of a lesson – and there are scores of them, most not recorded here. I have offered some suggestions for helping you to deal with them. I stole some of these ideas, and thought up some of my own. If I was able to do it, I am sure you will be able to do the same.

5 Trouble in store

IN THE LAST CHAPTER I mentioned a few things which can take you off guard. I suggested one or two strategies for dealing with them. While you are doing the dealing, you can at least take comfort from the fact that they weren't your fault. Like the weather, they just happened.

But there are, alas, plenty of other situations which can arise, and which can give you some grief, and this time you can't take shelter behind being blameless. You brought them upon yourself. This time the curative strategies can be more difficult to think up and carry out. Why? Because the ideal remedy for these situations – the one you should have thought of –is never to have got yourself into them in the first place. And you do have some control over that. Like the 'safety' precautions on the box containing that glossy gadget you have just bought. Here are some things you *don't* do. Or at least shouldn't do. If you do, you won't fuse the lights or blow yourself up, but you could be letting yourself in for a good deal of long-term trouble.

They are in no particular order – and most of these injunctions could be applied to almost any circumstances in your daily life and work, so they are not revolutionary. Put the other way, they are not peculiar to teaching. However, some might be more likely to arise in teaching because you are an adult dealing with young people.

For instance, don't show off.

It is so bemusingly easy. You have more knowledge than they have. Of course; you have passed all those exams to get degrees and diplomas. Even simpler, you have been alive longer than they have; you must have picked up all sorts of skills, knacks, tricks, wrinkles, and wisdoms that they haven't. It is a very human desire to want to demonstrate that fact when the chance arises.

Unless you are particularly wet behind the ears, you are more savvy than they are. Because of all that, you are more confident than they are. There will be times, of course, in front of a fresh class, when you feel nervous, but generally speaking and on the whole, in the general business of living and dealing with the world, you are more confident.

If you do feel nervous, then the temptation to show off and bolster your self-esteem becomes that much stronger.

Beware.

For several reasons. Here are two.

One: life is cussed. Whatever little prodigy you attempt, it is extremely likely that it will go wrong. If you are in any doubt, don't. The advice is as old as the hills. I bet Aesop must have written a fable about it. If you ignore the warnings (consciences are rarely stupid) and go ahead, and you slip up, it is not just a simple mistake; you are in soup up to your ears. Worse, it is something you brought upon yourself. And serve you right.

Understate. Lay off. Shut up.

And two: even if your little performance does come off, it isn't worth it. They may be impressed by what you have done, but they will not be impressed by the fact that you have given in to the temptation to do it.

They will know at once what you have been trying to do, and they will know why. They can smell swagger and swank a mile off. Perhaps because they have learned, after much practice, to spot it in each other.

You will have slipped. It can take time to clamber back up again.

Being tempted to show off is one very common human weakness. Getting cross is another, even more common. In fact, it's universal. Even Jesus got cross.

What makes it difficult to handle is that the urge is stronger. If you show off, it is because you think, rightly or wrongly, that it is a good idea. Getting cross doesn't imply that you want to. Indeed, you know that you shouldn't. That sensible conscience again.

All the more reason why you should do your best not to. The trouble is that, in teaching, possibly more than in most other callings, you are going to feel like it. My word, you are going to feel like it.

You are putting yourself out there, in front, in the lead. And you won't have willing allies at your side all the way. Never forget that you are there in the classroom because you want to be. They are there because of an Act of Parliament.

In that classroom, you will be smitten by every emotion in the dictionary – impatience, bafflement, uncertainty, confusion, shame, exasperation, surprise, embarrassment, worry, disbelief, frustration, even perhaps fear and despair. No doubt more too. They are all dragons astride your path to the Nirvana of admiring attention and total control.

It is up to you to try and control them (the dragons as well as the class). But you know that you will show signs of all of them in varying degrees at one time or another. You are human.

Make your greatest effort, though, to avoid showing the slightest chink of another one – temper. You can hide nearly all the others, up to a point. It is difficult to hide temper.

That is the greatest giveaway of all. Then you really

have let down the drawbridge. At a stroke they can see that control has been lost. You have appealed to the very worst in them. They can see at once what they have to do to produce the same results.

It is to be hoped that you don't get difficult pupils or difficult classes, but we all know that sooner or later you will, and there are likely to be some monsters among them. When they see temper, that's when their eyes begin to glitter.

If it gets really bad, and you can't think of anything to do, if all else fails, walk out. They may be a little surprised; they may even be a little mystified. That's good. Either way, you have unscrewed the tension, and you have retained the initiative. What is 'Sir' going to do? You have them just a little on the hop. And they have seen that you have taken a positive decision, and not, for instance, slapped anybody's face or broken down in tears.

Moreover, you have given yourself space; they can't be rude to somebody who is not there. You have given yourself time – to calm down, cool off, think of something. Even mere physical movement can be conducive to creative thinking. Staring eyeball to eyeball isn't.

Once the immediate crisis is over, you have the chance to think about it from a longer perspective. All right, you have lost your temper. Find it – pretty damn quick. You have left a hole in the dyke. Mend it – also pretty damn quick. Work out what you did wrong, what you hadn't planned for, and put into place some ideas and practices which will help to prevent it happening again.

Don't hope for miracles. You are not going to turn them into saints. Not on two periods a week. They are not the ones who should reform; it's you.

That should give you something to think about. Don't beat your breast about past mistakes; concentrate on future successes. When you do, aim high, of course, but don't expect too much from yourself. As I just said, don't expect miracles. Just something which is do-able. By you. And by them too.

While you are about it, don't expect perfection either – not in yourself, not in them. Because if you do, you are on the edge of another pitfall. (My goodness – what a troubled trip in life you have chosen for yourself.)

This time, the pitfall can yawn in front of you not because you are careless but because you are trying. Too hard.

Don't nag.

Yes, you want to show that you set high standards; that's splendid. You should always try to get the best out of them. That's splendid too. Not perfection, but the best they are capable of. That's not only splendid; it is sensible and realistic, and much more likely to produce success.

Chase them, get after them, insist on regular effort – yes, yes, yes. Set an example yourself. Yes again. That is not difficult; all you have to do is what you are expecting them to do, and trying to *get* them to do.

But there is a limit. It is the difference between the bottle being half-empty and the bottle being half-full. It's balance. Show them when you're dissatisfied, by all means. But you must show them when you're satisfied as well. However hard a taskmaster you are, you must be pleased sometimes. Tell them when they are close to failure, but tell them too when they are close to success. Everybody enjoys turning round and surveying what they have achieved. Give them something to look back on.

No pupil – even the one who doesn't give a damn – enjoys failure. Moreover, regular failure. He can perhaps live with disapproval; there are plenty of other teachers, neighbours, probation officers, and possibly magistrates who can give him that. He can tell them all to get lost. But failure is a different matter; failure is in his head – it doesn't go away.

Worse, he doesn't want to be constantly reminded of it. Worse still, having it proved to him.

Don't yap at their heels. It means that you're behind, moaning, instead of in front, leading. By that time, they won't be listening anyway. Nags are always a nuisance, never an inspiration.

In my work as a school archivist, I once read a letter written by a parent to his son in a boarding school at the other end of the country. This was from the prehistoric days before computers, mobiles, Facebook, and all the rest. In the whole school, there was only one public phone. Pupils relied totally on letters.

The last paragraph read like this: 'Lets [Father had omitted the apostrophe] have a few more capitals, full-stops and better spelling in your future letters, please.' It was typewritten, even the 'much love' at the end. Though he did have the grace to sign it with a pen.

This poor lad was young, he was separated from his family and home for months at a time, and he was over two hundred miles away. What he wanted from his Dad was news about the coming Christmas, the funny thing that happened when Mum took the dog for a walk, a word of affectionate reminiscence. He couldn't care less about the bloody full-stops. I submit that Father was in effect a nag.

If you asked anybody whether he wanted to be a nag, nobody would say 'Yes', would they? It is self-evident.

But quite a lot of teachers, if they spoke honestly, would like to be popular. I daresay we nearly all do. It is a rare person who does not favour the idea of being liked.

All the experts tell us that the greatest gift you give to a child is love. We need to feel that somebody likes to have us around, whether it's somebody Up There or somebody down here. (Preferably both.)

There is no need to get sentimental about this, and one must maintain a sense of balance. The classroom is not a crèche. But at the very least, most teachers would like the comfort of knowing that their pupils are reasonably pleased to have them there.

The problem then, if problem it is, is to work out ways of achieving this highly satisfactory state of affairs.

It is no crime to be popular; it is no sin to enjoy being popular; it is no black mark to aspire to being popular.

The paradox is that popularity is one of those things that you can't achieve by wanting it, or by trying to get it. Like happiness. It's a much more roundabout business. Ultimately, the state of being popular comes about from them, not from any effort by you.

Niceness doesn't work. Broad smiles don't either. Being the soft touch, the willing shoulder to cry on that is too often there, generous favours – no. Worse, lavishing attention on 'deserving cases', offering 'friendship'. A thousand times no.

What the hell do you do then?

You wait, that's what. First of all you work out that popularity is only the dividend, and it can not be guaranteed. The market is as volatile as it is on the Stock

Exchange. Young people are unpredictable; there's no knowing what they will do, and life can be hard.

What you do during the wait is build up the investment. *Your* investment. And remember that the dividend is proportionate to the depth and the genuineness of that investment.

Come on, come on – what's the trick?

No trick. It's work. God knows, there's enough of it waiting to be done. So get on with it. Don't keep cocking an eye to the popularity polls. The evidence will show. You'll find out soon enough. In a hundred microscopic ways – a sudden smile of chance greeting in a corridor; a cheeky remark which is only made when a pupil feels comfortable; homework coming in on time; offering to do tiny favours, and it is clear that nobody is creeping. You'll find out all right.

I have stressed that the secret is not being nice. It's not being nasty either. You know – the dragon, the tyrant, the beast from outer space.

You don't have to BE anything. Just busy. Doing your best. Making yourself useful. Get it across. Make it stick. So that they know it. And remember it. If all that happens, they might, they might just, remember you.

If you are lucky, that's when the dividend comes – but, I said, there is no guarantee, and you may have to wait years before you find out.

A man once walked across a crowded hall in order to thank me for teaching him to write, over forty years after he had sat in my English class. All right, so it didn't prove that I was top of the pops, but somebody was clearly grateful that we had been in the same classroom together, and I'm happy to settle for that.

Finally, yet another piece of shriekingly obvious advice: don't break your word. As with some of the other points I have been making, this has to be modified in order to fit the context of the classroom. On its own, it sounds trite, almost precious.

Of course parents try hard from the earliest possible days to plant deep in their child's psyche the idea that the most sacred thing you ever give, to anybody, is your word. I don't mean that. Nor am a talking about courtroom oaths or Mummy's promise.

But the principle is the same, if only in a milder form. If you say something, it helps if you mean it. We all say things we may not mean when we are under stress, and a class lesson in full flow can breed stress, so a teacher has to be perhaps more circumspect than most.

In a classroom a teacher not only gives a lesson; he talks about other lessons. Future lessons. To put the lesson in context, to create interest, anticipation, publicity, whatever. Out come the advertised new schemes of work, the pious hopes for dazzling results, the intoxicating new ideas in the pipeline. Splendid.

The more numerous and the more glittering they are, the faster and harder those hopes can fall. The more the scepticism gauge rises. Be wary. Keep your language moderate. Don't get carried away. If you're not sure, don't say.

Incidentally, this applies particularly to threats, always a very dodgy way to secure co-operation.

There is an exception here. The lurid threat. 'Any boy who fails to hand in his insurance waiver form by next Monday will receive a hundred lashes.' It's outrageous, it conveys a certain sense of urgency, and everyone has a good laugh. It's a sign of a healthy atmosphere.

No. I mean something more serious than that. Put simply, they are sharp, and quick, to notice when you don't deliver. Very soon, yet another threat becomes a yawn. Be wary; once again, if you're not sure, don't say.

Once you have worked out the implications of what you plan to announce, and the circumstances in which you propose to announce it, then you go ahead; you don't need to threaten at all. You just do it. If you work it right, you should not need to threaten again. The message will have gone across.

But think it right through first, and make sure: are you really prepared to do it? If you mean it, they soon learn.

Five 'don'ts' then: Don't show off; don't get angry; don't nag; don't try to be popular; and don't break your word.

Any teacher with a dozen years of experience under his belt could come up with a similar clutch of warnings, and I'm sure they would be as valid as these. But this is enough to be going on with. Even good advice has to be rationed.

Any teacher or games coach reaches a stage at which he puts the ten commandments away and turns the pupil loose. No doubt to make more mistakes. The same applies to teaching diploma students. The best way to learn to do something is to do it. And mistakes are arguably the best training of all. Teachers can make you yawn; mistakes make you blush. Which are you more likely to remember?

So stick with it – the do's and the don'ts, the ups and downs, the advice, coaching, mistakes, blunders and blushes. Never fear; you'll get there.

And when you do, you will find that there is another

little surprise waiting for you: it's not the end; it's the beginning.

6 So now you're a teacher

WHAT IS A PROFESSIONAL teacher?

Sounds a simple question. We know what a teacher is and we know what 'professional' means. So, logically if nothing else, a professional teacher is a person who earns a living teaching in the classroom or the lecture hall or somewhere else public – or anywhere of course if he does it privately. He, or she – let me remind you again that, when I say 'he', I am talking about two people – he has a right to be styled, and known, as a teacher.

Words have a tricky habit of not telling you everything about themselves the first time around. Words, particularly the simple ones, often have implications as well as meanings. Anyone who loves cricket knows that 'a man who plays a bit of cricket' is not the same creature as a 'cricketer'. Similarly, a musician knows that a man who 'tickles the ivories' does not automatically have the right to call himself 'a pianist'. Well, it's a cheek if he does, and he'll show himself up before he has played a dozen bars.

Similarly with teaching. Imagine: you have studied your specialist subject, as likely as not up to university degree standard. You have studied further for the diploma in Education. You have survived the periods of teaching practice in proper schools with real live pupils. You have read the books, yawned over the esoteric articles in learned magazines, and you have passed the exams.

Is that it? No. Are you home and dry? No, you're not. From now on, everything will be different, even though it may not at first look different, and you will have to get used to it.

The minute the university Vice-Chancellor (or

whatever dignitary they have roped in to do the honours) puts that diploma in your hands, you cease to be a student. Richard Gordon, the author of *Doctor in the House*, summed up the thrill of becoming a doctor by pointing out that now he could sign prescriptions and death certificates, and mothers would trust him with their daughters. Newly-qualified teachers can look forward to making middle-aged men and women feel uncomfortable at parents' evenings and being called 'Sir' by an obsequious caretaker. (With luck by the pupils too.)

Well, if you're not a student any more, what are you? A teacher, of course. Technically, linguistically, as you might say, yes. But there are one or two procedures to be gone through and survived before you will begin to feel like one.

What you have just done is become a member of a profession. A very distinguished profession, up there with medicine and the law and the priesthood. Of your own free will, you have bought into an organisation which has its own rules and its own standards, to which you now owe duties and loyalties. You are not a free agent any more. It's like marrying into the Royal Family.

All sorts of things will change. Not much, maybe, to begin with. Not because of new rules and regulations. Not because of your willingness to follow the advice of experts. It will just happen. It will be because of the surroundings and 'climate' in which you find yourself. If you got a job in the tropics, sooner or later you would stop wearing Harris tweed and buy a bush jacket.

You will not embark on a campaign to behave in a teacher-like fashion, because you may have only a vague idea of what that is. But, as you edge into your day-to-day work, and as a result of a thousand tiny, unconscious decisions, your behaviour will start to change. You won't be able to help it.

As I said in Chapter Two, you won't revolutionise your dress (or it is most unlikely); but, over the months, you may take a lot of small decisions for purely practical and personal reasons, the cumulative result of which, over a period, may produce discernible changes.

Again, your language may, shall we say, 'develop'. Remember, you are not a student any more. You are now spending much more time in the company of young people. You will also spend time in the Common Room, in mixed company. You will be dealing more with seniors as well as with juniors and equals. Each circumstance demands your thought and attention, if you value the concept of good manners, that is. And we presume that you do. We presume too that you value the concept of example.

You will develop a 'teacher' voice. Teaching is not a conversation. Well, not in a classroom it isn't. There may be up to thirty people who need to hear you. You don't talk to them now; you address them. You are projecting something – knowledge, a mood, an atmosphere, yourself. Something. Otherwise, what are you there for?

A lesson is not a chat; it is a performance. Even if it looks like a chat, it isn't. Ideally, this should not show. You don't see good actors acting; you should not see good teachers teaching.

The trick it to make it look as if nothing much is happening. Watch a really good actor. Try and work out what he is doing. The Hollywood star Gene Kelly said he was glad when he was cast in a film with the legendary Spencer Tracy. He looked forward to studying him at work, and spent hours on the set, watching intently, even when he himself was not in the scene. By the end of the film, he said, he was staggered at the effect Tracy was able to achieve, but he could not for the life of him work out what Tracy had actually done. But he had obviously done something.

As in any other worthwhile activity, the best practitioners make it look easy. And that is the most difficult trick of all.

All that has to be learned. Putting the Vice-Chancellor's diploma in a frame on the wall and sticking 'Dip. Ed.' after your name are just the beginning. What do you actually do?

The time-honoured way is to watch the people who are good at it, as Gene Kelly tried to do. Or as Michael Caine said, 'Steal, but only steal from the best people.'

Which brings us to colleagues.

It is quite likely that you have never had colleagues before. You may be the most friendly, lovable, charming, outgoing, charismatic personality on the block. What you have had up to now, probably, like nearly everybody else, is a varied mixture of human company – family, friends, neighbours, team mates, club members, drinking buddies, morning coffee regulars, and I don't know what. You have enjoyed them, and you have contributed to them. Bully for you.

Colleagues are different. You can be as friendly, charming, likeable, and outgoing as you are with everybody else, but they're different. They are fellow-professionals. They merit a level of formality and correctness that marks your relationship with them as – I just said – different.

You may feel as warm and friendly towards them – well, some of them – as you do with family, friends, neighbours, and so on, but what marks the relationship is your shared membership of the teaching profession. And your shared respect for the profession too, for the work they do.

By the same token, if you *don't* like them, your attitude towards them must be equally correct. Your responsibility is to treat them as fellow-members of a profession rather than as human beings. Of course you treat them with humanity, kindness, and common decency, but always, at the back of the mind, must remain the thought that they are fellow-professionals, and as such are deserving of respect.

It is similar to the division of respect which Voltaire displayed in the quotation often attributed to him (wrongly, apparently): 'I disapprove of what you say, but I shall defend to the death your right to say it.'

By virtue of this correctness that you display to colleagues, you enhance your own image amongst the pupils too. If you want them to show respect for you, you have to prove that you yourself can show it to other people. At the same time, it raises your colleagues' stock with pupils, as your colleagues' visible respect raises your own stock in pupils' eyes.

Never forget that, from now on, in the environment in which you have chosen to work, you are important. There are few of you and many of them. You have joined the movers and shakers. Wherever you go and whatever you do, you are on show. From the minute you walk on to the campus in the morning to the minute you leave in the evening, you are on show. Once again, it's like being a member of the Royal Family.

It doesn't matter whether your natural modesty and self-effacing nature make you shy away from the idea. You should have thought of that before you started. There is no escape; it goes with the territory.

Think too of all the straitjackets you are putting on. Constant visibility; constant examination by hundreds of young eyes, who do not have the mature judgment of adults. You can be misquoted and misunderstood, and consequently unfairly criticised. Talked about. Gossiped about. Moaned about. Even complained about now and then. It is a long way from that scroll of fancy paper in your hand as you pose with proud Mum and Dad on the broad steps above the manicured lawn of the university senate house.

That is not the end of it. All that is simply what you have to put up with. There is also the small matter of what you have to do. Not as a student any more, but as a professional. Things begin to harden. Not so many allowances are going to be made. No more of the easiest classes. No more being let off special responsibilities. No fifteen-period-a-week timetables and 'time to prepare'. You are being paid a salary. Now you pull your weight.

Not just for a few weeks or half a term. Every day and every week. The time for choice is over. Teaching is no longer something you reckon you do fairly well when you happen to be in the mood. You must now deliver a level of achievement which does not fall short of a consistent standard, regardless of how you feel at the time. You have to know your job well enough now to be aware of when you are performing well and when you are not. And of course, if you are under-performing, to be able to knuckle down and think of something to do about it.

Remember too that there are other people in the classroom besides you – probably twenty-five or thirty of them. Waiting for you to get them going, and keep them going. Nobody has asked them whether *they* feel like it this morning. They have to sit there and do the work.

Well, you have to stand there and do the same. Every day, like the sun coming up.

If you do it properly, they come to rely on you, which if course is what you are aiming for. Well done.

It's a nice feeling, to be relied upon. But that in turn brings its own problems. The more you deliver the goods, the more they depend on you to carry on delivering the goods. It can become second nature to *expec*t you to deliver those goods. So you reach the stage whereat the higher their expectations, the greater the pressure on you.

It's like the bright pupil who makes a habit of coming top of the class; the more often he does it, the greater the expectation that he will continue to do it, and the more he feels the need to make the effort to ensure that he does. If you're top, there is only one way to go – down. Not an ideal situation. Those who do not come top, but who merely aspire to, do not understand that pressure.

What I am saying in a roundabout way is that teaching is tiring. It is a fine thing to gain the diploma; to be offered the exact job you wanted; to take on board all the good advice contained in books, articles, and lectures like this (if you find any); to catch your pupils' interest, get them going, win their respect; bask in their success, and all the rest. But it comes at a price.

However naturally gifted you may prove to be, success in teaching comes at a price. Success in anything comes at a price. So many outsiders tend to assume that success makes it all a doddle. No, it doesn't. Generally speaking, the one who comes out top has been working harder than all the others. Even if you make it look easy, it isn't.

Too many wordy critics of teachers and teaching are inclined to base their judgments on casual glances through the transparent pane of glass in classroom doors as they go past, and on their imperfectly-recalled experiences of their own schooldays.

They select and they simplify. Many do not even observe correctly. There is more to it than saying: 'Get out your text-books and turn to the exercise on page 71.'

OK. So you get tired teaching. But don't you get tired doing any job if you do enough of it? Yes, of course you do. But my agenda is about teaching, not about every other job, and I want to do two things:

I want to correct the impression, often widely held, that there is not much to teaching really. This may have come about because, as I said above, we have all seen teachers at work, close to. And, because we were young, we may not have fully understood what they were up to. Unfortunately, because everybody has been to school, everybody is an expert on education, and knows exactly what needs to be done to put the educational world to rights. Just because you know all about being on the receiving end, it does not mean that you know all about dishing it out.

I would like to offer a few suggestions as to how a young teacher – any teacher – can make teaching not quite so tiring.

Pacing it is one idea. The less experience a teacher has, the shorter his perspective. The probationer has so many things on his mind – preparation, finding his way around, learning names, remembering to set homework, keeping order, locating board markers, and the rest – that he'll be grateful when he gets to the end of the lesson, never mind the end of the week or the term. He has been pouring out nervous energy by the gallon. And there are probably six or seven more periods in the day to come. And it's only Tuesday.

Look ahead. Marathon runners don't start like a bull at a gate. Teachers shouldn't start as if they are going to solve all the problems in half an hour. Think. Work out the time when you will have to work harder than others, and conserve your energy accordingly.

Don't expect too much of yourself. However young or old you are, you have a finite fund of nervous energy. Ideally you should be as fresh on Friday afternoon as you are on Monday morning. You won't be, but at least you have a target, an approach, an intention, a hope.

Think of all the things that might affect your disposition: several late nights, too many things to get done in the lunch-hour, a heavy marking load on a particular day of the week, how to transport several piles of exercise books, a heavy lunch just before a tough lesson in an over-centrally-heated classroom. There are dozens.

Learn to spot the symptoms: dragging yourself out of bed, shortness of patience, more reluctance than usual about taking that awkward class, less backchat with colleagues, no time to catch up with the news, cutting corners – the list is like Marley's chain of cash-boxes.

From daily-increasing tiredness to the beginnings of depression is a short step – when it all begins to get gloomy. That wretched girl is not just a 'pain' – she's a threat; you can't wait for Friday; God, there are three whole weeks to go till Easter; when you're not sure you even did the right thing by going for a damn diploma; are you in fact up to it. You follow the general idea.

So butter yourself up. You wanted to do it in the first place. You haven't really changed. You know that not many people want to teach; you're unusual. Even, in a way, special. A lot of young people may be somewhat sceptical about you (yes, no doubt a few somewhat hostile too), and a fair percentage don't care much one way or the other, but they mostly accept you for what you are – a teacher.

That means that you are in a position of power, privilege, and trust. All the time you are there, and probably a few places outside too. That means that you have to live up to it. Don't blab; don't gossip; don't judge; don't sneer; don't mock; don't surrender to sarcasm. In other words, don't abuse your power and status. They have no protection, no means of retaliation. All they can do is dislike you.

It makes demands on the character, yes. What is wrong with that? Do you want a job which makes no demands at all? Presumably, you rate your character strong enough to live up to those standards.

To repeat, you are now in a rare position. You know perfectly well that you should do nothing to abuse that position. When you come to think of it, you are rather lucky. That's quite an opportunity you have been offered. Take it. All you have to do is nothing – nothing which might reflect discredit on yourself, your colleagues, your work, or your profession.

7 Pious hopes

THERE ARE SEVERAL CALLINGS which appear to imply that the practice of them involves a measure of sainthood. Missionary is an obvious one. Care home assistant is perhaps another. Teaching is arguably a third. They all suggest that the practitioner does not put himself high in the list of priorities. As opposed, say, to the young aspirant who wants to be an actor or a Formula One racing driver. The one is willing to sacrifice; the other is thirsty for triumph.

Such people do not see themselves as particularly saintly. Joan of Arc wasn't trying to be a saint; she saw her life simply as obedience to her 'voices'. Virtue didn't come into it; she felt she had no choice. St. Augustine frankly didn't want to be saintly at all. He famously asked God, 'Give me chastity and continency – but not yet.'

With people like that, it was the work that mattered, not the soul.

It is the same, I fancy, with setting out to teach. The keen ones – and we hope, don't we, that the vast majority are keen, or they wouldn't be there – are burning to *do* good; not to *be* good. They are realistic enough to know that they have their share of human weaknesses, and they set out do their best in spite of them.

It is just that they can go overboard in their eagerness to do that spot of good as they pass along. They can get things just a little out of kilter. Oddly, St. Augustine was alive to that. He said, 'To many, total abstinence is easier than perfect moderation.' So his lust didn't get in the way of his common sense. Pretty good going for a saint.

Put another way, young teachers, being keen (and a

good thing too), arrive with a brief case brim full of good ideas and good intentions, which they are eager to put into operation. They may run into trouble because they have not, as the wiseacres would put it, 'thought it through'. Of course they haven't; they don't have the experience which provides a longer perspective to enable them to do it.

As with our introductory missionary, they want to spread the word. Devotion to the virtue and logic of the 'word' can blind them to the fact that classes of pupils may not be quite so aware of the same truth.

One of the first lessons a probationer learns is that the teacher presides at a desk, not a pulpit.

If times have changed since I did my first year's teaching, and young teachers are now so worldly, savvy, sensible, wired in, clued up, and on top of their game that they don't need the next bit, well OK. You may not need it, but there may be just a few poor benighted souls out there who are prepared to read it, if only out of curiosity. The Ten Commandments are still, if nothing else, such good value in themselves that nobody would recommend taking them out of the Old Testament. After three thousand years, they still have something to say, most of which is difficult to disagree with.

However, unlike Moses with those ponderous tablets under his arm, you are not there to tell them what is right; you are there to tell them what they want to know. Don't worry about the 'righteous' bit; just being yourself will tell them what you think is right. Every move, every glance, every phrase, every reaction, every scrap of body language will tell them that. Because it's you. It will be happening, be well assured, without your trying. You probably won't even know. Never fear; it'll go across all right.

If you try too hard to *put* it across, you will fail. The minute they sense preaching, the yawns begin and the shutters come down. They don't want to be done good to. Even if you're right, you're wrong. The classroom is not the time or the place.

So much for the pious intent. What about the dream? That you, the class, are all going to share in the great adventure of learning. That you, the teacher, are going to lead them out into the sunny uplands of knowledge, understanding, and enlightenment, and they will all follow joyously, like the children of Hamelin after the Pied Piper. Before long, they will become so inspired and uplifted by this crusade of yours that they will be only too eager to contribute to – nay, share in the leadership of – this mighty quest.

It doesn't work quite like that. The classroom is not a salon; it is not a forum; it is not a debating chamber; it is not a symposium; it is not a club drawing room. *It is an arena.* The abiding ambience in a classroom is a semi-permanent state of friendly undeclared war.

Whether you like it or not, you are the ringmaster. Without you nothing will get done. You may not want to be cast as a boss or a dictator – very praiseworthy. But you must recognise that the initiative lies with you. They accept that. It has to be you who calls the shots. They accept that too. If they could lead and educate themselves, they wouldn't need teachers. Even in the adult world, where most people treasure what they see as their independence, it can often be comforting to be told what to do because it saves the trouble of thinking and deciding. A crowd in a sudden crisis will listen to (and frequently obey) a strong, decisive voice.

Moreover, young people need leadership. So it still comes back to you.

But surely, there must be times when their voices have to be heard. Yes, of course. This is where the common sense, gumption, and St. Augustine's moderation come in. Plus, perhaps, something out of a teacher's little armoury of secret weapons – low cunning.

Teaching, when you think about it, is a bit of a con. Education takes some selling. (Hence the 'friendly undeclared war' I spoke about. That is their resistance to the selling.)

For instance, there is a difference between saying, 'This Friday you will write a new type of essay,' and 'This Friday we'll have a crack at a new type of essay. Don't worry; it'll be quite painless.'

Anything can help – humour, soft soap, wheedling, jazzy advertising, They know the whip is in your hand all the time, but you haven't had to crack it. It's a fair cop.

In that war, both sides accept that there is room for compromise. Neither side can expect constant success. Things don't go right all the time. You win some and you lose some.

That is realistic, and pupils appreciate realism – or what they see as realism. It gets you along the track. You get through the work. When they look back at what they have done, there is an element of satisfaction.

Good. You have managed not to pin your hopes too high. It is much better to be gratified by unexpected success than depressed by unexpected failure. Keep your hopes to yourself.

We have come to that feature of the human psyche which is generally known as 'better nature': that nebulous facet of our humanity which we are so often enjoined to appeal to in others. Not in ourselves, oddly. (How often do the advice columns tell us to appeal to our own better nature? Do we assume that we have one? Or that we haven't?)

More to the point, do young people have 'better natures' that we can appeal to in order to obtain their co-operation in our quest for the perfect lesson?

The cynics of course would at once say, 'No. No such thing. The teacher's job is to drive things into them, not tease things out of them. If they do in fact have better natures, that is their business, private, and nothing to do with the classroom. Whether they do or not is none of *our* business. It's a straight, simple set-up: *you* teach, and *they* learn. Full stop.'

Well, it's a point of view, and I'm sure it has not been arrived at lightly. And many holders of that view can make effective teachers.

Whether the young teacher – or any teacher – has a right to seek more is debatable. Does it come under the heading of pious hopes? What is your chance of getting it?

I don't know. (One of many questions raised in these chapters to which I don't know the answer. All I can do is follow Socrates: not answer the questions; just ask them.)

One thing, though, I am fairly sure of: you won't get much of a glimpse of better natures if you come straight out and ask for them. That is not the way they operate. In fact, of course, they are as human as the rest of us. They have better natures all right, but showing them has to be their idea. They don't want to be sweet-talked or black-mailed into it.

It's like the case of the boy/girl who comes up to you in the playground or the dinner queue and says, 'Will you be my friend?'

No. They don't want niceness and good-turnery put into their heads; they want to be left to think of it themselves.

When they do – and don't expect it to be often – they can take your breath away with their perception, kindness, maturity, and general good sense. But, I repeat, not often. The common or garden pupil is an animal of rare and infinite variety, not staled by custom. Capable of depths as well as heights.

Your average pupil, then, besides having its share of original sin, has its own store of inscrutability. In order to maintain a balance, it behoves the teacher to have his own share of it too.

Whichever metaphor you like – don't put too many cards on the table; don't let down too many shutters; don't let them get too close (worse still, don't *invite* them to get too close) – your primary intent should not be that they get to know you better and better. It's a class, not a club. You can be a well-liked, trusted, highly-respected, even revered mentor without being a friend. There should always be that last little ditch of mystery and unknown quantity.

You may bark, and they may well accept the barking and understand the goodwill behind it. However comfortable they feel with you, they have to know that somewhere in the background there is a bite. You don't have to employ it – well, certainly not much. Just so that they know it is there. Use your own methods. The best ones are unconscious, because they spring from your own personality. Once again, don't dwell on it. You are often at your best when you are not thinking. As I have already said several times (and will probably say again), simply getting on with it.

Be yourself and do your job. And see to it that they don't know absolutely everything about you. That would mean that they have gone right through and come out the other side. Gone with the mystery will be a lot of the interest.

There was a television personality years ago – a lady of formidable intelligence and presence – who was asked in a panel show whether she thought her husband understood her. She replied almost in a state of shock, 'Good Heavens, I hope not. If he did, he would leave me tomorrow.'

However many similarities there are between adults and the young, and however much *camaraderie* that produces, the maths remain. There is a gulf. Perhaps the young are more aware of it than their elders. However much they may want to appear and behave older than they are, to be thought of as 'grown up', there is a built-in resistance to the adult who tries to cross the same divide, and come to them.

The young are intensely suspicious of anyone who appears to be asking for a level of intimacy deeper than they feel like giving at the time. Yet another situation in which the teacher must take great care to tread gently, to keep back, to lay off.

This reaction seems to be shared by all pupils, the good ones as well as the bad ones, the workers as well as the idlers, the saints as well as the sinners. They are all prepared to accept that school is a place of work – even those who don't like it, and those who don't do much of it. But that is all.

Well, now, let us review the situation. You have listened to the advice, read the books, done your stuff, kept up with your marking and your beauty sleep, and collected as much experience as you possibly can. So how good are you? How well, and how accurately, can you judge yourself?

Whatever conclusions you come to, you will by this time have come across teachers who you think are better than you, and those who in your (private) opinion are worse. So you have a few yardsticks. Being human, you would like to get better yourself.

I should think so too. So this is another of what you might call pious hopes. 'Pious' does not imply criticism. Simply the suggestion, as I said earlier, that you may, from an excess of desire, try too hard, and so frustrate the achievement.

If you join the local cricket club, you can not, in normal circumstances, expect an early letter in the post inviting you to come for a county trial.

When you start teaching, you soon come across reading matter which discusses national awards, special features on young celebrity practitioners, courses for improving professional practice, and so on. Sooner or later the concept of the ideal teacher swims into your ken.

Well, let it.

But concentrate your attention and effort on doing what is immediately in front of you. That way, you learn to work out, and – we hope – accept the sort of person you are. Don't allow yourself to be bewitched by the idea of Supersir or Supermiss. That is a pious hope run wild. Very few of us, by definition, are Supersir or Supermiss material.

(How do you judge it anyway?)

The teacher isn't born who is good at everything. Falling short of 'Supersir' status simply means that you are not the best in the country or the county or whatever – as judged by a panel of 'experts' who are human like you.

You will learn that you have both strengths and weaknesses. Build on the one and accept the other.

If, for instance, you are not good at cracking jokes, don't crack 'em. There are other ways of getting your point across. If you are not bursting with charisma and charm, don't try to charm them. If you are good at humdrum detail, at dotting i's and crossing t's, then dot i's and cross t's. Thoroughness is a precious virtue. They will come to rely on you to do that, and will respect you for it.

Don't let other people's success press you into a feeling of inferiority. They succeeded because they were good at something (we presume – although sometimes we wonder, don't we?). Well, you're good at something else.

If it turns out that you're not much good at anything to do with education, then you have some thinking to do, for your own peace of mind, never mind their welfare. And the sooner the better. It still doesn't make you a second-rate human being. On the contrary – a very sensible, honest, and resourceful one.

If you are imaginative enough to consider the possibility of failure, you are also imaginative enough to consider the chances of promotion.

In this case the 'hope' may not be particularly 'pious',

but it fits this argument closely enough to merit inclusion in this chapter.

It is a rare teacher who finds that, with that Dip. Ed. still crisp in his hand, he has dropped into the perfect role in the perfect school in the perfect locality, and that it satisfies all his aspirations.

The vast majority of us, sooner or later, want a change – up, down, sideways, (or out of course). The 'down' element may seem a surprise, but there are plenty of cases of teachers who, for a variety of valid reasons, seek planned demotion. I have worked with two ex-headmasters who, so far as I could see, had an enjoyable career back in the classroom after leaving the top spot. I didn't delve into their reasons; that was their business.

But of course most of us want to move up, or at least sideways.

This book is not a guide to successful promotion. Heavens, if I'd known all that, I would have had a very different career. All I can do is point out a few of the issues involved, and wish you success.

It is a good idea to work out clearly what your motives are, and make sure they are positive and realistic. That demands a fairly high degree of self-knowledge.

As with teaching itself, do your homework. Make sure you know what you might be letting yourself in for. See to it that you are as free as human character permits from negative factors. Such as? Well, escaping from something (remember the frying pan and the fire); self-sympathy; envy; a chronicle of bad relations with colleagues or authority. That sort of thing. There is a danger it will come out if someone asks you searching questions in interview (if you get that far).

Never be ashamed of hopes, even the pious ones. A lot of good can come out of them in the end, usually in the form of experience. No experience is ever wasted. Try and use all of it to make yourself comfortable. If you are comfortable, so are they. A classroom does not have to be exciting – just satisfying.

8 Scraps of solace

HEAVEN KNOWS, THIS BOOK is well sown with simplicities and obviosities, but here is one that beats them all: *things will go wrong.*

So what is the point of saying so? Certainly not to inform you; you already know that. Unfortunately, teachers starting out in the business do not have the experience and resilience possessed by their elders and seniors. When something does go wrong (as it inevitably will sooner or later), they react more strongly. They take it harder. They can get more upset. They can take it more personally. From there it is a short step to the feeling that you are the only teacher in the whole world who has ever suffered from this painful proof of a capricious deity stalking you. From there again it is an even shorter step to the conclusion that you have somehow brought it on yourself, almost certainly through your own inadequacy, and that capricious deity has cruelly brought you face to face with it. Even rubbed your nose in it.

The object of this chapter is to provide a few crumbs of comfort, a few rescue tactics, a few warming truths, a few first resorts as well as a few last resorts. Maybe even a few shrugs and a few fatalisms.

First: don't clutch your temples. Remember Corporal Jones' immortal advice.

Don't fret about it; just set about it. Use your common sense. Your particular trouble is hardly likely to be unique in the annals of the magisterial profession. Countless thousands before you have had to face it. The overwhelming probability is that they worked out how to deal with it. If they managed it, so can you.

Sit down – afterwards – and think about it. Exactly what happened? Look at the whole episode, from every angle – your preparation, the complexity of the topic, the wrong questions asked, unfortunate remarks thoughtlessly dropped, careless handling of an awkward pupil, a silly verbal clanger of your own, trying to get too much done, having too little to get done. The list could go on: the size of the class, the wrong pupils sitting together, the wrong spacing between the desks. Even the weather might have played a part. Think, for example, of the effect of a high wind. You can easily add a further dozen yourself.

Of course some things went wrong. But I bet some things went right too; you can't be that bad. Already you have started on your way towards a solution. Take comfort from the fact that at least you are not going to make that particular mistake again. If you are, there is possibly something wrong with your technique, and that will need some attention. If you expect them to correct bad habits or bad practices, you should be prepared to correct your own.

So you got some things right and you got some things wrong. What does that prove? Nothing much, except the blinding truth (yet another blinding truth) that you are not perfect. You should have tumbled to that by now. With luck, and a spot of honesty, you should also by now have a fairly good idea of what the weaknesses are. If you are lucky enough to have a friend or colleague you trust, you could invite him or her to pass comment on what they have seen of you in action. I had a colleague who often recorded various History talks I gave to a local audience of village neighbours. As he was putting away the plugs and wires one evening, he said, 'One thing, Berwick. I hope you don't mind. But you have a habit of jingling coins in your pocket while you are speaking. If you do it a lot, it can become a distraction.'

He was right of course. And he was being kind. I clearly *had* been doing it a lot, and it *was* a distraction. I had had no idea. Well, that was an easy one. All I had to do was make sure I had no coins or keys in my trouser pockets when I stood up next time. And I had to suppress the blushes at the thought of how many times I had done it in the past. That water was under the bridge, well on its way to the sea, and it wasn't coming back.

Things like this can afflict you so easily. Only recently I listened to a lady lecturer who had a script that she hoped to hold us with for an hour and a half. To her credit, it did, and her material was important and relevant, and she was right on top of it. But she had wayward long hair which persistently blew or fell around and across her face. She was forever pushing it away or tossing her head. The movements could have been in danger of becoming hypnotic. I know nothing about feminine coiffure, but wouldn't a couple of pins have helped?

One word of wariness, by the way. When you ask someone a question like this, you have to be sure that you are prepared to hear the answer. If you have had a mentor allocated to you for your probationary year, you can feel freer about asking him. That's what mentors are for. Already, then, you are not alone.

Now, those weaknesses are likely to be of two types, aren't they? Those that you can do something about, and those you can't. If you can do something about them, get on and do it. Keep a little of your own judgment in reserve, to assess the value of what advice you are given.

Remember your friends, colleagues, and mentors aren't perfect either. Before you accept any advice from anybody, no matter how experienced or eminent they are, it has to make sense to you. You are going to be the one out front doing it, and taking the punishment if it goes wrong.

If the weaknesses are of the second type, it would appear that you are stuck with them. All you can do then is bumble through and hope that you might get a bit better; or avoid the occasions at which these situations are most likely to arise.

For instance, if you once allowed yourself to get roped into producing a class play, and it was a disaster, don't ever allow yourself to be talked into doing one again, no matter how much the Head of English lays on the soft soap or flutters her eyelashes at you.

Or you may have discovered that you are more at home with older pupils than younger ones. Possibly you will have a clutch of flattering exam results to back you up. (It is a rare teacher who is equally at home at both ends of the age scale.) You can't tell the Director of Studies how to do his job, but you are free to go to him and make a case. You never know.

However, at the end of it all, you may have to live with the weak points, the *bêtes noires*, the blind spots, the chinks in the armour. So what? You are not Confucius or Pallas Athene. Don't dwell on them. Work on the good points. Play to them. Try and create situations in which those good points are more likely to be shown to better advantage. Even if some of your good points are odd ones, they are yours. Other people may not have them. (Yes, we know; they probably won't want them.) Be proud of them. The more you put them to use, the greater your chance of success. With growing experience, you will be able to use those strong points to manufacture situations in which you are in a good position to succeed. The more often you do that, the more your confidence will grow. That can be transmitted. A teacher's confidence in himself transmutes into comfort and co-operation in the class.

You are not selling perfection; you are selling yourself.

In that sales campaign, you are not alone, like John the Baptist. Admittedly, there may be times when, with a particularly bolshy or Philistine class, you may feel like a voice crying in the wilderness, but we all have moments like that. Even parents may feel like that now and again with their children. We know that better moments will come round.

Think where you are operating. In a school. It is chock full of desks and pens and paper and laboratories and workshops. A school is a place dedicated to 'work', to learning, to education – *by definition*. The whole atmosphere, the climate, the total ambience is on your side. Dedicated to learning. The naughtiest, the stupidest, the worst-disposed pupils know that. They may not like it, they may try to avoid it or challenge it, but they do not dispute the sheer fact.

Because a school is a complex human unit, it has a network of authority to enable it to function.

So everybody accepts the fact of its existence, and its entire structural anatomy is based on authority. Of course you are not alone.

It follows then that if you find yourself plagued with difficult pupils who make work impossible, there is an organisation behind you and around you to back you up. It is no weakness to use it. That's what it is there for.

Nobody expects a mere lieutenant to run the army. If he could, there would be no need for generals.

Keep a sense of balance by all means. Don't run for cover every time there are a few drops of rain. Give yourself credit. And allow yourself the opportunity to learn from adversity. But you also have to learn to recognise the occasions when the weight of the problem is greater than your lowly authority can bear. That is not weakness; that is good judgment. Being a member of a profession does have its advantages.

Another comfort is that, unless you have landed in a uniquely anarchic school where they are only a couple of scandals short of closure, you will get help from people who have themselves been where you are now. People who understand, people who want you to succeed.

If there aren't any such people available, then all is not lost. The school itself is part of an even greater hierarchy, going right up to the county education committee and the Chief Education Officer. From then on, the county – nay, the country – is awash with agencies which, if suitably stimulated by the justice of your cause, will take up a cudgel or two on your behalf: school governors, educational psychologists, trade unions, the press, the law, members of Parliament, ombudsmen, and I don't know what. You've got company all right. Whether you will want to get involved with them or not – possibly over a long period – is another matter.

That is what is going on all around and above you. Now consider what you yourself have to offer towards a solution. After all, the overwhelming probability is that the problem in question is of pretty lowly significance in the overall scheme of things. A couple of bloody-minded little show-offs in a lowly class in the local comp. Or a set of lessons which went well enough last year, and are not ringing the bell this year. Or confusion created by a badly-planned timetable (which was probably entirely someone else's fault).

We are back again to the 'avoid temple-clutching' advice of the first page. Survey your own position. Time to do a little asset-counting.

You have been alive longer than they have. You must have more experience. Experience of what? Nothing in particular – just 'Experience'. It must count for something. You have read more, studied more, passed more exams. You have degrees and diplomas and things. You might even have gleaned a smattering of educational psychology. You have at the very least a nodding acquaintance with the educational system of the United Kingdom. If you have managed all that, it would appear to indicate that you have a few brains.

You have a useful bunch of cards in your hand. Well, use 'em. Think of something. Don't expect dazzling success, certainly not at the first go. Don't expect *total* success either.

It doesn't have to be a brilliant 'solution'. It doesn't have to be a masterly strategy. Just a tactic, a ruse, an idea. Maybe only a desperate last resort. But it's a step forward. Even if it fails, it could trigger a better idea, which you wouldn't have had if you hadn't tried the first one.

Another suggestion. If you find that a particular problem is spending too much time on your mind, find a way of taking it off. Don't gnaw at it. Do things which demand virtually no mental effort at all: gardening, a favourite hobby, an athletic passion, reading airport paperback novels, watching junk television films. Anything which stops you brooding on it. Even a drink, a fatty cake, and a good sleep.

If it is a particular pupil, or group of pupils, who are disturbing you, virtually the same technique applies. Don't waste time dreaming up scripts and scenarios in which you emerge triumphant and they are completely discomfited. It never works out like that. You are on a jag. Get back to the garden, the old LP collection, the Disney films, and the jogging (it's difficult to stew about something when you're puffing hard and pouring with sweat).

Incidentally, I used to find that it helped to divide the 'run' into four. Part one – you're cold or stiff, or plain unwilling. It's hard work, and it's slow. Part two – you get into a rhythm, the muscles are lubricated, and you begin to feel that you might, you might just, get something out of it. Part three – it's going with a swing; you are taking note of your surroundings, particularly enjoyable if you can do it a rural setting; you can even get creative ideas. Part four – you feel you have achieved something; the end, the shower, the armchair, and the cup of tea are on the horizon… and it's all been worth it. Just an idea.

When you are right up against it, and feeling perhaps a little powerless, it is easy to forget that you do in fact have quite a lot of power – in a general sense, all the time.

As I said, you are older than they are. That has an effect. They may be difficult, argumentative, rebellious, critical, all sorts of things, but you are older (they can't get away from it), and they all want to be 'grown up' too. They want to look adult and be thought of as adult. They have no idea how an adult thinks, any more than a thirty-year-old knows how a pensioner thinks. So all their attempts are guesswork. But the desire is there. They will watch you, and form judgments. Whether they like it or not, you influence them. That is a useful thing to be aware of.

Then of course, besides the question of influence, there is the question of authority. A school, as I have tried to make clear, is a hierarchical world. The teacher – you – have a firm, and vital, place in that world. I spell it out once again: you have power.

Most of this chapter has been about snags and difficulties and nasty surprises, and I have tried to console you with the fact that – for a third time – you have power. Do not be afraid to use it. Indeed, there will be times when you use power not to get yourself out of trouble, but simply to keep the place running. So power becomes not only a rescue tactic but a duty. Like an officer insisting on being saluted.

It is your job to be powerful when necessary. Power, though, is a devilish tricky commodity. It has a touch of addictiveness about it. It's easy to get used to it. Particularly when you have to exercise it every day, as teachers do. It is easy to slip from using it as a rare resort to falling back on it as a routine reaction. Teachers are in a uniquely convenient position to be able to use it. Think of how easy it is to nag, to sneer, to scorn, to bully, to over-chase. You can doubtless think of more. Quite possibly recall when you were the victim of them. The memories will not be good ones.

Power puts you in a privileged position, which can be dangerous. It is the greatest intoxicant of all.

But let me not conclude on such a dire note.

I hope I have maintained a balance between pointing

out pitfalls, and indicating that there are remedies, or at least resorts you can try – with no guarantee that they are infallible. There are no magic spells in the classroom. But I offer hope and comfort. And, I trust, some realism.

It has to be do-able, otherwise nobody would want to become a teacher. But it is not easy, and there is no assured success. If you really come to think that it is beyond you, then you need to consider the possibility of leaving the profession, and it is no disgrace. If you feel teaching is worth a try, fine. Have a go. If, thirdly, after reading some of the literature, and having nibbled round the edges, you come the conclusion that it's a doddle, the chances are that you haven't yet dug deep enough to discover the difficult parts.

I once shared a common room with a brainy young man with two degrees, and who had fancied he would like to give teaching a spin. After a week or so, he confided to me, 'Here, this is money for old rope, isn't it?' He had been given the youngest classes, to be on the safe side.

Before we reached half-term, they were eating him alive.

9 Asking questions

WHY ASK QUESTIONS?

It's one of those awkward primary-school Year 3 posers, isn't it? Like 'Why is the sky blue?' or 'Why do teachers put a tick when a sum is right and a cross when it's wrong?'

It's almost as basic as 'Why work?' or 'Why be nice?'

There are almost as many imperfect answers as there are people, and it won't necessarily enhance your career if you happen to come up with a good one, but I suggest that you may be a little better off for giving it some thought now and then. It is useful to have a response to a question like this, however far from perfection it may be. It shows that you have faced the simplest features of what you are doing – which are often the most difficult.

So think about it for a moment. It is impossible to contemplate the process of teaching without giving some attention at some time to the phenomenon of questions.

My goodness me, where do you begin? What follows is far from systematic, and certainly not exhaustive.

Why do teachers go in for questions? Well, for a start, it's a means of exercising control. You can't beat a well-constructed question session for gaining and keeping attention. You are proving that you know more than they do, always a useful advantage. By framing and aiming your questions carefully, you can open up for them a realisation of how much more they have yet to learn. Anything which shows a pupil that he doesn't know it all has to be a good thing in that semi-permanent state of friendly undeclared war that I spoke about. You are not cracking the whip, but you are twitching it.

It does not have to be like a session with the Grand Inquisitor. A good questioner makes his effect with the content of his questions, not with the manner of their delivery. I had a colleague who had just joined the staff, fresh from receiving his diploma. He was a Physics teacher. Naturally, he made it his business to watch his head of department in action, if only to find out what was going on. This gentleman was a middle-aged, slightly absent-looking, almost vague, quietly-spoken practitioner, but with considerable experience.

This young teacher said to me one day, 'You know, it's difficult to work out what Charles is up to, and how he does it. He never raises his voice, but, when he is running a revision session, every boy in that lab is sitting on the edge of his stool in case Charles asks him a question.'

That has to be good technique.

Ideally, we need at this point a chapter (written by Charles himself) to explain his method. But we haven't. We have – or you have, if you're inexperienced – a clean slate to work on, with the questionable backing of a willingness to learn. Willingness of the teacher, that is. In the case of the pupil, it is more likely the willingness to show what he already has learned.

In your favour is the human desire (they can be very human sometimes) to show off their knowledge. Ask the class as a whole, and quite a few will be keen to tell you. Especially the younger classes. Nothing more encouraging than a small forest of raised hands. If the questioning is person to person, the pressure is that much greater. Added to the desire to show off is the relish of the challenge of wits. (If there's one thing they like for light relief at the end of the term, it's a quiz. Well, it always has been in my experience. And think of the number of quiz shows on the box.)

This may be an over-optimistic view. By the law of averages if by nothing else, there will be one in the class who doesn't give a damn. You can carry him. You can possibly carry two or three. But when the numbers begin to rise, it will be time to think. If the first session was a flop, time to think of ways to avoid another one. There is no future in a procession of questions followed by silences – worse, silences accompanied by smirks and sidelong glances. Don't bang your head against a brick wall. Think of something. Doesn't matter what it is so long as it's different. Come at it from another angle. If nothing else, it might take them by surprise. At once, the initiative has passed to you. Good. (I nearly said 'passed *back* to you'.)

I shall not pursue that line, because this chapter is about questions, not about alternative strategies.

Let's take not a general approach, but a particular one. Specifics. What *sort* of questions do you want to ask?

Is it to get them to remember? Good idea. You may get a surprise or two when you find out how much has sunk in. An even bigger surprise, perhaps, when you find out how much hasn't. Which puts the ball firmly back in your court.

If you arrange your questions to follow each other in a sort of logical progression, it gives them help in working out what might be coming next. If you want to make it harder, then of course you cast progression to the winds and toss questions at them from all angles. It's the difference between getting them to recite the whole of the four times table and asking what eight sevens are, then four sixes, then three nines.

It is good practice to frame your questions so that there is only one possible answer. Read them through the day before. Try them out on a willing family member.

Now suppose you want not merely to make them remember, but to make them think. Incidentally, you can sometimes catch them on the hop with this. It is so easy for them to get used to routine questions and routine answers; they are at risk of reaching the stage of doing it almost on the automatic pilot. That means you are getting short on surprises. Your resources are getting low.

Beware surprises yourself. If you ask them to think, you have to be prepared for unexpected answers. This is uncharted territory. Experience well teach you the 'normal' unexpected answers, but you can never be sure that there isn't a real googly waiting round the corner. If it really does bowl you out, then you have to pick up your bat and retire. But do it with a good grace, and they will understand. You will have helped to establish a bond of humanity. A good laugh works a treat.

Whatever you attempt, whatever you have in mind, good question sessions don't just happen. It always comes back to preparation. The best performers prepare, prepare, prepare. Tommy Cooper, with his tricks that nearly went wrong, was a compulsive rehearser. Actor Anthony Hopkins said in an interview that, by the time he was ready to go in front of the cameras, he had read the screenplay over a hundred and fifty times. Top-flight performances, whether in the classroom, on the stage, in the courtroom, on the athletics track – anywhere – are never chancy.

Better still, they can see what you have been doing. If they can't see it, they can sense it. It shows. Like those circus animals under the ringmaster, they can sense control. They will respond. Like Charles's Physics students on their hard lab stools. (Don't forget that they can sense loss of control too. It's like radar.)

How much have they remembered? How much have they forgotten? How much *should* they have remembered? There are other intentions. It may be to make them develop a respect for the topic or the subject, to show up gaps that they didn't know they had. With a class that has its tail between its legs, for all sorts of possible reasons, it may be to boost morale; to show that the subject is *not* beyond them. It is not simply about turning the sentence around and sticking a question mark on the end.

This may apply as much to individuals as to whole classes – probably more so. You could find yourself applying all sorts of principles as you move round the classroom and fire your questions.

A class is not composed of identical pupils. It doesn't matter whether you worship at the altar of Mixed Ability, or whether you believe in segregation under a dozen different systems related to age, sex, religion, racial origin, geography, estimated ability, proven ability, or anything else. Pupils in a class are different, no matter how much you 'organise' them. You get to understand this with every lesson you take with them.

Pupil A is shy; don't behave like a prosecuting counsel. (Remember that this session is in front of everybody else. Who likes their ignorance shown up in front of other people?) Pupil B is unsure of himself; make sure that the first question you ask him is one that you know he can answer.

I once had a lad in an English class who was cheerful,

well-behaved and amenable, but his goodwill was being eroded by regular failure. He was clearly not in the least academic, and, from his record and my knowledge of his background, he wasn't going to get much academic support from his home surroundings. His family were not in the least anti-education; they just didn't have the wherewithal. This boy badly needed a success, or I was going to lose him. So when I set a homework in which the class had to learn a set of spellings for a test the next day, I gave him a different set to learn – within his range. I forget how he performed. That does not matter. What mattered was that he felt it was do-able, and he had a go. For years afterwards, when we met in the street, he would remind me of this, and tell me all over again how much he appreciated it.

This was not gifted teaching or ground-breaking brilliance – just kindness and common sense.

Failure when you don't care doesn't keep you awake at night. But frequent failure when you want to succeed is murder. And it's often so public. If a girl gets flustered by having to say 'I don't know' two or three times in a row, she won't be able in the end to tell you her own name. Watch contestants collapse in *Mastermind* if things go wrong

If pupil C is a cocky little devil, make sure that one of the early questions you ask him is something that he *can't* answer. Pupil D probably knows the answer, but it takes him a little bit longer for the message to get from the brain to the tongue. And so it goes on. You can no doubt thinks of other examples. I'm not surprised. Most of what I have been saying here is not revolutionary, original, or complicated. But I may be offering a truth when I remind you that a question session may involve several of these problems/issues/ difficulties, and arising at the same time.

You have to be aware of the variety of the people in front of you. You are tackling human nature. Some are more withdrawn, some are more pushy, some are more sharp, some are more slow off the mark (*by the standards of that class at that time*). It is not a case for the mindless routine. It is fatally easy for a teacher to forget this, ironically the more experienced he becomes. I have actually caught myself in mid-lesson churning out the same old material. It was a slightly different context, but the point is relevant and valid. I could actually hear myself, and it sounded so boring. I felt sorry for them. I felt like saying to myself, 'Berwick, why don't you shut up!'

Take care what you say, take care who you say it to, and take care how you say it.

The same watchfulness should apply to your material. If you have done it umpteen time, that is all the more reason why you should give thought to some way by means of which you make it sound just a little fresh. Don't ask the same questions, either in writing or in speech, time and time again. Try and vary it just a bit. I have known of teachers using the identical revision test for years, regardless of whether they have covered exactly the same ground as the questions refer to. It comes out when pupils complain that the latest revision test asked questions on subjects which they had not dealt with at all. Pupils enjoy a good moan like everybody else, yes. But this time it looks as if they have caught you out being plain lazy. Not good for morale or for teacher-pupil relations.

With a question session, you have to be right on your game. You must do your homework. I apologise for insulting your intelligence, but practise some of the questions, even when you know the stuff backwards. I have said this elsewhere, but I'm saying it again: because, through usage, it has become simple and easy to you, it does not follow that it is easy to them. Or even that making it easy to them is easy.

Have a think. Are there any questions that you can re-phrase to as to make them easier for them to understand where you are going, or where you are coming from. If some of the questions are part of a particular sequence, make sure that that sequence is clear.

Some question sessions go badly, so that you will perhaps need some fresh material. Some sessions will go well, and you fly through the agenda. So once again you will need fresh material. Always have a reserve. It is a terrible let-down, when you have worked up a momentum, to find that you have run out of fuel.

The lesson does not have to be frantic, like a TV million-frame-a-minute commercial. Speed doesn't prove anything. Concentration does. It must also have pace, and it must have purpose. No gaps, no hesitation, no let-up. Like that Physics teacher, don't give anybody a chance to switch off.

If you can pull this off, the pupils will feel the pressure; they won't be able to avoid it. They will feel the urgency. You achieve this by feeling it yourself. You must ooze adrenalin. Adrenalin is catching.

It's pretty concentrated too.

Just think what you are doing. Think of all the processes that you have set in motion beforehand, and that you are about to set in motion now.

You have decided when to have a revision session. Early in the week? Later? A morning period? An afternoon one? When are they at their sharpest? If you hear on the grapevine that a fire alarm is about due, try and find out whether it's likely to scupper your plans, and react accordingly.

Decide the topic and range of your questions. What are the aims, the limits? The point? The purpose? What do you want to show, or to prove? (If anything.) Do you plan to spring it on them, or do you want to drum up a spot of drama and urgency?

Think of the range and type of the questions you plan to ask. Look again at the points I made about the targets for your questions, and the tailoring of those questions. While the session is in full swing, you have to keep your eyes moving, to catch anyone showing signs of switching off. And so on and so on. If you do it properly, I suggest you should feel tired after five or six minutes. And they should feel that something has happened. That's what teachers are supposed to do – make things happen.

You never reach the end of talking about questions. So I thought I would round off this imperfect survey with an anecdote. (You should build a little larder of anecdotes.)

I had a colleague (another colleague) who for years taught elementary Latin to the bottom class (in this case Year 7). Latin is not the sort of subject that makes twelve-year-old boys clap their hands in anticipation, but Tony Prichard ('Prickles' to one and all, which tells you something about him straight away) had worked up a breezy technique which carried him through many a struggle with declensions and conjugations.

He met the problem head on. He made no bones about how difficult it was. In fact he laboured the point. He warned of dire retribution for poor performance.

Hyperboles flowed thick and fast. He gave his forthcoming revision session a lot of advance publicity. It would not be merely a big one; it would be 'mammoth'. As a special 'treat', he would prophesy that very soon there would befall an even bigger one – a 'Hairy Mammoth'.

Pass by his open door any day, and you could hear a snatch of conversation like this:

'Are we having another test on Tuesday, sir?'

'Yes. Of course.'

'Is it a hairy one, sir?'

Talk to any survivors of his lessons for decades afterwards, and you would hear fond reminiscences of 'Hairy Mammoths'. Never a grumble.

He showed me a letter he had received from a boy who had had to change schools. He wrote to describe his new school, paying particular attention to the Latin lessons. After 'Sir's' regime, he said, it was a piece of cake.

Now, a hard-to-please reader may feel doubtful about the strict relevance of that story, but I put it in, not so much to illustrate the business of conducting revision sessions (though I hope it helps a bit), but rather to show what can be achieved by a teacher when faced with getting across a subject which is not noted for its popularity. 'Prickles' achieved his success with honesty, humanity, and humour. Three unstoppable weapons.

10 Teaching and trust

THE PROBLEM IN TEACHING is to induce a set of young people to spend up to forty minutes at a time (sometimes more), close together, on hard seats, in a bleakly-decorated room, in proximity to an adult they don't know from Adam, to listen to what he says and to do what he says (when they may not understand it, and quite possibly not like it) – and moreover to put their backs into it.

Quite a tall order. Put like that, it would be unlikely to attract many people to the profession. So it would appear that there is more to it.

This is typical of the glib, snap summary that anybody with a smidgin of wit can come up with if he puts his mind to it. The cynic's over-used weapon.

You could concoct a similar squib about any activity. Hunting has been described as 'the unspeakable in pursuit of the uneatable'. Cricket, to a man from Mars, would look like a group of grown men in odd clothes hurling, beating, and chasing a leather sphere round an enormous lawn.

All good for a tolerant light chuckle. Is that all? I suggest no. Cynics don't tell lies, but, as the gentleman said, they can be economical with the truth. Nevertheless, some truth lurks there. If it didn't, the comment would be worthless. But how much truth?

Anybody who goes in for teaching will see more in it than this cynic has suggested, but it is useful once in a while to ponder what he has said. We are down to the basic, basic question: just what the hell are you doing there, what are you selling, and how do you get them to buy it?

I am concerned with the third part of that problem. That is what faced those who first stood, on their own, in front of a roomful of young people. Not all that long ago. It is easy to forget that a nation-wide teaching system in England is only five or six generations old.

Yes, there were schools before that. Up and down the country – the famous public schools and the venerable town grammar schools (my own school boasts a pedigree going back to 1272). But they were not typical; they did not reflect what happened to countless millions of ordinary young people between five and eighteen over the centuries. The truth for these children was hard labour in the home, the farm, or the workshop. To boost the family economy. They may or may not have been loved, but they had to contribute. Every penny counted. Very little was spare.

Families grew children because they were potential work units. It was the concept of 'education' which suggested that it might be a good idea to invest in their minds, not merely to train their hands.

This is a crudely simplified survey, but there they are – the bare bones. With the cloudburst of rising population after the late eighteenth century, the educational pioneers were faced with large classes and few teachers. So few that they simply used older children as teachers (there was nobody else). 'Monitors' or 'pupil teachers' became common currency. Think of the limitations of such a regime.

That was part of the problem. The other part was control. Look at the first paragraph again. Classes could be forty, fifty, sixty strong. Just what do you do?

People did what had always been done. What choice

was there? Early teachers were not noted, any more than anybody else, for originality. It was fear and violence. That was the traditional way; in the opinion of many, the practical way. A lot of them and one of you. What else worked? (No wonder they thought Jesus not so much wrong as impractical and unrealistic.)

Priests threatened Hellfire. Masters whipped their apprentices. Heretics were burned at the stake. The armed forces used the lash. Husbands, we are told, often beat their wives. Rare, liberal-minded parents who didn't believe in inflicting physical punishment on their children could be, and often were, regarded as cranks.

This attitude had become enshrined by time, tradition, and custom. It was not cruelty; it was common sense. The biggest priority was order. This concept took a long time to change. Even when many of the population became sceptical about religion, society was careful to replace that fear with another one: fear of Hellfire was superseded by fear of the scaffold; at one time over 200 offences could carry the death penalty. All in the name of order and the protection of property.

A system so entrenched took a long time to be modified. Here is not the place for a potted history of educational theory and practice. But modified it was, as we know. In the schools, the cane and the slipper are long gone. Learning by rote – endless recitation and chanting – is rare. Simply having more teachers around helped. Pupils and teacher have time and opportunity to think. One of the trump cards in the independent school's hand today is 'smaller classes'.

All right. So a teacher today does not beat them; he does not bully them; he does not blackmail them; and he does not scare them. Being nice doesn't work either. With the fear gone, inches freely given are met with yard-taking. Human nature. Comfortable, well-fed pupils today, freed from fear and poverty, are no more angelic than an apprentice of 1746 or a page of 1368.

So beating is not allowed. Being nice, on its own, is asking for trouble. How about sheer knowledge? That doesn't work either. Even if you overcome the hypnotic effect on them of trivia, ephemera, and the lowest common denominator, and actually get them willing to listen to culture, that is not enough. They will admire you, but not much more. It might get them to cock an ear, but it doesn't get them to mind.

Admiration, liking, even respect, on their own, don't cut the mustard. What does?

I put this forward with all due diffidence and tentativeness, but, so far as I am aware, nobody has yet come up with a better idea than trust.

How do you achieve that?

Start with self-belief, I suggest. Quite a lot of self-belief, actually. You have to believe that you can do it. Diffidence and modesty don't cut the mustard either. This is where classes can be hard.

You have to feel that, if somebody were to ask you the straightest of all questions, you could reply, 'Yes. No kid; I really think, deep down, I can do it.' This is no time for gazing modestly at your toes and hoping that somebody will come along and take your hand.

Not only believe in yourself, but believe in what you are doing. Believe that it is worthwhile and valuable, and deserves respect. At my college, there was a sort of steward, you could call him, I suppose; he ran the college shop, close to the dining hall. Students coming out of lunch or dinner could pop in and buy all sorts of useful 'tiny' things – coffee, chocolate, string, shoe polish, you know the sort of thing. An account was kept, and the total was added to your college bill.

Bill Cornwell had presided there for so long that he was part of the college architecture. He was 'Bill' to everybody, high and low. He prided himself in getting to know the name of every student, and there were over four hundred of us. But that was it; he ran the college shop.

One day the Master of the College had some unexpected guests. This man was, I think, the most distinguished person I have ever met face to face. He was a Nobel Prize winner; he was a Life Peer; he was President of the Royal Society; and he was a member of the Order of Merit. And of course, as I said, he was Master of a prestigious university college.

On this day he was caught napping; there was no drink in his pantry. However, he knew what his guests' favourite tipple was, and Bill's shop was only thirty yards away. So he popped over and asked Bill for a bottle of gin. (Like everybody else, he had an account too.)

Bill duly provided it. The Master picked it up, thanked him, and was leaving, when Bill said, 'Excuse me, Master, but where are you proposing to go with that bottle?'

The Master, caught in the doorway, explained rather shamefacedly, that he was taking it back to the Lodge for some guests.

Bill drew himself up and said, 'Master, so long as I am a servant of this college, no Master will be seen walking across to the Lodge carrying a bottle. Now you put it down on the counter like a good gentleman, and I shall see that it is immediately delivered.'

And he did. And it was. The Master told this story himself, and clearly relished it. He had grasped at once that, with Bill, it was a question not of insubordination but of pride. Each man respected, understood, and trusted the other. Faced with this personality of towering eminence, Bill felt sure of himself.

Tony Prichard, from the last chapter, had this similar self-belief. If you believe strongly enough that what you are teaching is worthwhile, you don't have to apologise for it. If you feel it, you transmit it unconsciously; it's not difficult. Prickles' classes were not nuts about second declension passive verbs, but they were happy to go along with him. He sold it so well that they bought it.

Curiously, liking the subject is not the paramount ingredient in the mix, though of course it doesn't half help. But it's the breeze, the passion, the confidence. If the truth were told, I don't suppose Tony put irregular verbs and indirect speech at the top of his private likes. Actually, his passion was opera (though I doubt whether he would have found many fans for it in a class of twelve-year-olds).

What Tony had succeeded in doing was what every teacher should try to achieve, to make a particular penny drop: namely, that if an activity makes a person confident, keen, and happy enough to stand in front of a class every day and plug it, there must be something in it.

I repeat, not so much in the subject matter as in the procedure, which, for want of a better word, we call 'education'. Here, perhaps, we get close to an appreciation of the old aphorism that 'education' is what we have left after we have forgotten everything we learned at school.

It is not something you spell out. I doubt whether you

can. You just get it across, and you often don't find out whether you got it across till years later. Teaching requires patience for a variety of reasons.

All right, so you have convinced us; trust is wonderful. There are hundreds of lovely stories about pupils trusting teachers. But we are not all memorable characters like Tony Prichard. We are not all bursting with charisma. We are not magicians; we are ordinary.

That's all right. Trust, like love or loyalty, is not something you create by a wave of a wand or sheer brilliance. Trust does not descend in a blinding revelation like some Pentecostal gift of tongues. It is not an arcane mystery accessible only to a gifted or favoured few.

Anyone can do it. Anyone who wants to be a teacher, that is. It is routine, it is ordinary, it is unspectacular, it is humdrum, it is day-to-day. You just do what you are supposed to do. You all know what that is. In a sense, it is what I have been going on about right through this book.

Anyone can build trust so long as they are prepared to build it brick by brick, tick by tick, mark by mark, lesson by lesson, day by day. Every minute counts, in however gradual a way. What the philosopher (I forget his name) called 'the inevitability of gradualness'. You'll get there.

All you need is a stone and a regular dripping pipe.

Like a watermark living in a quality sheet of paper, running through all education is the idea of repetition. It is not the *only* idea, of course, but it's an important one. More important, perhaps, than many people would give it credit for. It would be easy to underestimate it because it looks so mundane, so underplayed, so apparently un-creative. So crushingly boring. Oh, no, we can't teach like that. They'd walk out.

No. Teaching is not an endless procession of great moments, brilliant coups, memorable aphorisms, mighty principles, side-splitting jokes.

Teaching, on the contrary, is very ordinary indeed, like laying the table, cleaning your teeth, doing the chores. In the end, you don't notice them. The only thing about them that you would notice is if they weren't there.

The same with teaching. The edifice of trust you are building consists of a thousand small, unobtrusive actions, which, I say again, anybody can do. Remembering to set the homework; returning the marking on time; finding a chance for a quick pat on the back (it doesn't have to be an embossed testimonial – just enough to show a boy or girl that you noticed).

Simply noticing – is a pupil quieter than usual? Less willing to offer replies. Trying to understand why another one is having trouble; being kind when someone needs a leg up; explaining again when they don't get it the first time. It's little more than common sense. So ordinary, like a great deal of what I have said elsewhere. You can work out lots more for yourself.

The more you think of them, and the more often you do them, the better it gets. They don't get bored with it; they don't even notice it. But, over the weeks and months, they are getting comfortable. They can't help it. It's so easy to get comfortable. Nevertheless, you have to create the atmosphere in which they can do it.

Don't get precious about this, whatever you do. They don't talk among themselves and assure each other that, 'Gosh, we are getting to trust Sir so much, aren't we?' Rubbish. They don't sit down and work it out. They don't know what's going on. All they know is that, at the very least, it is quite acceptable.

I spent fifteen years working in a comprehensive school. Like most other staff, I had a tutor group. It was the usual bag. Well, with a comprehensive school, it would be, wouldn't it? There was one girl there I remember – let's call her Wendy. She was bright – no genius, but bright. Happy too. She was prompt, she was polite, she was smart – a credit to any school and any family. In fact, I remember writing once on her tutor report: 'The best compliment I can pay this girl is to say that she has never needed me.' I also taught her, and her record was identical in class.

Then, one morning, Wendy came into the tutor room breathing fire and brimstone. There had been an incident – I forget what it was – but everybody knew about it, and everybody was talking about it. She had got the impression that another member of the tutor group had been unfairly treated, and it seemed that I was responsible. She came straight up my desk, with eyes blazing, and, without any preamble, said, 'You can't do that.' She was a girl of such normal even temperament that her wrath was formidable.

Luckily, I was able to convince her that I was not to blame, and that no great injustice had in fact been done. A close shave for 'Sir'. But the real moral of the story is that she was clearly cross, and in effect said so, unmistakably, yet she felt confident enough in our relationship to say what she said without fear of reprisal. She didn't stop to think. There was injustice, and she spoke out. On my side, I knew her well enough, and I was sure enough of her character, not to take any offence. I like to think we both came out of it with a certain amount of credit. But the real hero of the story is trust. We both trusted each other.

I have stressed in this piece that what the teacher has to do is not difficult, but he has to work at it. Secondly, building trust is a two-way business, and the pupil must show willing too. You can't do it with a roomful of puddings. Which of course throws it back to the teacher's wit and initiative.

He evolves his formula. He works steadily, unobtrusively. Water on a stone, as I said. Repeat, repeat, repeat. Patience, patience. The inevitability of gradualness. Eyes open, wits sharp. Get through the work. Little things. Lots and lots of little things.

If you get things done, they will come to trust you; and if they trust you, you get things done.

What you are doing is strewing as much evidence as you can in front of them, and trying to make sure that all that evidence is in your favour. The jury, we hope, will have only one conclusion to come to.

You are selling something you believe is worthwhile., and you are using trust to get that something across. If you are successful, it is quite likely that the relationship you build will turn out to be stronger and more lasting than the subject matter of what you have been trying to teach.

All those boys in 'Prickles's' classes have probably long forgotten Caesar's campaigns in Gaul, and the Neuter Plural of the noun '*bellum*', but they will all take to their grave their memory of his Hairy Mammoths.

The prospects can be made to look rosy, but ultimately it is all up to you. Nothing is guaranteed.

11 Professionalism in pupils

IN THE PREVIOUS CHAPTER, I tried to take the argument right down to the basement essentials: just what the hell are you doing there? I suggested a sort of 'apology', if you like, about what a teacher was up to, and why he was up to it, and how he hoped to achieve something. Imperfect, no doubt, but it is not a bad idea to have just one or two answers ready to offer when somebody asks you in effect to justify your existence, and to explain how you propose to go about it.

After all, if you have nothing to say in such a situation, people might wonder.

Still talking basics, it is well to remember that in this equation there are two factors – teachers and pupils, dishers-out and lappers-up, 'you' and 'them'. Both involved in this extraordinary process we call 'education'. And they are different. The very fact that I say 'you' and 'them' means that it is not one great big unilateral enterprise.

Do both sides want the same thing? The very fact that I use the word 'sides' indicates opposites. Do they react the same way? Are they both going the same way? Do they both *want* to be going the same way? Are they both coming from the same place?

We are talking about motivation and aspiration. (Or, in some cases, perhaps, the lack of them.) Because it is the teacher who has to lead, who understands the problem in the round, who is responsible for trying to make the 'system' work; he is the one whom it behoves to try and understand the other. Pupils have no responsibility to understand the teacher. He is the potter; they are the clay.

This may all sound a mite woolly. All I am trying to

say is that it is not up to the pupil to think all this out; it is up to the teacher. I repeat, the pupil does not see this the same way. The teacher is in the classroom because he chose to be; he worked hard and devoted a sizeable slice of his young life to getting there. Two years for 'A' Level; three years for a degree; another year for a diploma. That's nearly 30 per cent of his whole existence to date.

The pupil is there in the classroom because of an Act of Parliament. Nobody asked *him*.

So what does being a pupil mean? It means lumping it. Same as they have lumped everything else so far. Did they choose education as a full-time activity after studying all the available prospectuses? Did they choose their school, their class, their teachers? Did they choose every subject in the curriculum? In the early years, did they choose *any* subject in the curriculum?

If it comes to that, did they choose their parents, their brothers and sisters, their home, their town, their country, their physique, the colour of their hair – anything?

Looked at like that, it's one long chronicle of putting up with it. Hardly surprising that they have a scream about it now and again. They don't understand how and why they came to be where they are. They have so little to go on.

The probationer teacher has much more experience of life, even at twenty-two, so it's not so difficult for him. He soon realises that joining the profession at once imposes limitations, rules, required practices, standards, expectations. A whole multi-layered cocoon of straitjackets. He learns not to kick against these constraints, because he knows he won't become a proper teacher till he appreciates the reason for them and respects them. This is called becoming a professional.

If, after giving it a fair go, he finds it intolerable, he can always leave. The pupil can't. Well, he can't without letting loose a squad of advisers, counsellors, social workers, child guidance experts, and educational psychologists.

The pupil has around him a similar cocoon of constraints. His learning to accept them in effect imposes a set of disciplines on him which amounts to a kind of professionalism. Pupil professionalism. Most pupils come to accept this, without being aware of it in so many words. Such acceptance and tolerance, I suggest, command a certain level of respect.

So much in education goes both ways. From teachers to pupils, and back. They can be a trial at times, a burden, a pain, (but we hope not a cross). How often do we pause to wonder how much of a trial we can be to them? With our eternal syllabuses, exercises, homeworks, revision tests, deadlines; our ever-present demands for more effort; our incorrigible hard-to-pleasery; our oddities, our funny tics and habits, our repetitions, our predictabilities – the list can be endless. Heaven help us if the whole class wrote thirty individual reports – honest reports – on us…

'He thinks one explanation is enough. Doesn't he realise we're the third set, not the geniuses? We're the thickos. We don't get it the first time. Probably not the second time either.'

'If he says "OK" once more I swear I'll throw something at him. In yesterday's Maths period, he said it a hundred and twenty-nine times. Didn't learn much Maths; we were too busy counting.'

'Somebody ought to tell her about that bra strap.'

'He's an ex-boffin. Get him on nuclear fusion, and you can put your books away for the rest of the lesson.'

'I'll never get full marks for dictation. She thinks we're all bloody short-hand typists.'

And so on and so on.

In this chapter, I have talked about 'you' and 'them', about 'sides', about criticism and frustration, about opposites. In a previous chapter I likened the classroom to an arena.

We all know that, in the ideal learning atmosphere, all is harmony, joint purpose, shared conviction and effort, teamwork, and mutual respect. We all know too that ideals are hard to come by. As teachers, we soon learn that while all this is being aspired to, there is going to be a pretty hefty share of unwelcome factors along the way. These can perhaps be lumped under the heading of conflict and impact. But we know too that it is conflict and impact which produces sparks. These are the prizes which make the game worth the effort. As in so many other enterprises, we need both – targets and obstacles.

For pupils the 'game' implies somewhat different rules. In no particular order, they are daily classwork, regular homework (what bane of the pupils' profession invented homework?), studying subjects you don't like, studying subjects you're not good at, being drilled and grilled most of the working day, sitting in lofty rooms on hard furniture, being polite to people you may not like or respect, obeying rules you object to, and several other things I've forgotten.

Sometimes too you can feel that not only is the game against you, but the referee too.

It says a lot for the average pupil's good humour and general goodwill that he is willing to play this game, and to go on playing it for a long time. However, if he happens to be a philosopher, he may also wonder what 'use' the whole damn thing is. Think for a moment how he might see it in his more reflective moments.

Is he going to be taken in by the threadbare adult argument that education does you good? Like taking your medicine, and going to the dentist regularly, and eating your greens? Who wants to be done good to all the time?

Then they play the 'character' card. You know – 'discipline, hard work, keeping the rules'. Well, OK. But by now somebody should have found better ways of developing our characters besides keeping us behind a desk five or six hours every day. So is that going to wash?

Thirdly comes the common sense ploy: 'You will need all that education to get you a good job.' Oh, really? How many of us are going to get that 'good job' because we know a lot of dates, or we love blowing up test-tubes, or we can't half play netball?

And how much of all that wonderful education is going to be any use to us when we know we will have forgotten most of it by the time we are twenty-three?

Take Physics. How many of us are going to be professional physicists? Music. How many of us are going to study Music after leaving? Play a violin? Queue up for an opera? Modern Languages – how many us plan to spend most of our future holidays in Spain or France? Even if we do, how much Spanish and French are we going to speak when we're sunning ourselves beside the pool or flogging up the Eiffel Tower? History – how many of us are remotely interested in the fourteenth century?

And God! Maths! How many of us want to spend the rest of our lives doing Maths? How many of us want to spend one more *week* doing Maths?

How many of us will remember twenty per cent of

any of all this five years after we have left? Dammit – how much are we going to remember for that wretched revision test next Tuesday?

If you, the teacher, become aware of some of the thoughts like this which whizz around inside pupils' heads, it may not make you smarter, but it may help to make you cannier.

If you find yourself presented with any of them, it may help too if you can offer some kind of response. It won't amount to a complete refutation of their objections, but it may give them a titbit or two to chew on.

For instance, school provides company. Maybe not ideal company; they will probably be a right mixed lot. And every pupil knows that he, or she, is the only completely sane and reasonable person in the whole school. But that company is the only company around, so he or she had better make the most of it. Lumping it again. Learning to lump it.

Something else they learn to lump is you lot, the teachers. Different teachers need different handling. The skill is learnable. Pupils learn to deal with human nature. They are learning to cope with a day chock full of appointments. They are learning to juggle deadlines. You can get this across too.

If the school is half well-run, there will be people there who know their job, and can demonstrate how to do it. You can be one of those people. Pupils will see how a dining hall can be well organised; how a sports team can be well coached; how a choir can produce good performances. If you do your job properly, you, the teacher, can be part of showing what the phrase 'good standards' means. You will teach them to recognise second best when they see it.

This is all part of your understanding them, over and above what you get into their heads about quadratic equations or the French Revolution. It is about helping them to understand the whole 'game' I spoke about. Helping them to play the game. Encouraging them to go on playing the game. If you're good, being aware of those pupils who are not playing the game, and putting out effort to get them *into* the game.

What is happening? It turns out in the end that though you are indeed peddling knowledge, you are also selling education itself; you are selling the game. In a sense that 'game' becomes more important than all the teacher stuff that will slip out of the other ear in the end. This is the bit that stays in. (You hope.)

It is asking a lot of a pupil to be 'professional' like this, and he has to take a lot on trust. You have to persuade him that it is all worth it, and that it will all make sense in the end; it will all work out. For your sake, it had better.

12 Putting yourself across

IF YOU HAVE EXPLAINED knots to a scout group, given a life-saving demonstration, acted in a play, or been on the giving end of a hundred similar activities, you will know what it is like to be watched. If you haven't, the first time you stand in front of a classroom of pupils can be a memorable experience. Even if you have, it will still be a strain. There is something about a classroom that is not there in a drill hall or a swimming bath or a theatre.

In those circumstances, your audience has come to be instructed, trained, or entertained. It's their idea. It's not the same in the classroom. (I made this point in the previous chapter.) Yes, you know they are listening in the drill hall, the swimming pool, and the theatre.. Well, they should be; they chose to be there. And you know they are there, of course. But in a classroom, it's more palpable than that; you can almost *feel* they're there. It takes some getting used to.

Young people's eyes are selective, but they are sharp. They may not see everything, but what they do see they see with laser-like clarity.

I read somewhere that this statement is literally true: there are some things that they physically do not see. The mind shuts it off. There was the story of the police searching for the driver of a stolen lorry. He had parked briefly outside the playground of a primary school before making his getaway. The police quizzed the children, naturally, about both lorry and driver. The boys supplied information about the size and make of the lorry, its colour, its condition, and so on. The girls had nothing to say about the lorry, but they had plenty to say about the driver – the colour of his hair, the ring on his finger, his clothes, the sound of his voice, and more. Each 'half' simply did not see what the other half saw.

There is also the famous experiment with the gorilla in the game of basketball.

Well, pupils notice things. And it doesn't seem to have much to do with the quality of the lesson or the calibre of the teacher. The good teacher of course is memorable; he makes it easy. But one can make the case for the poor teacher too. They see just as much with him. Maybe more; they are so bored; there is little else that grabs them.

Good or bad, turned on or turned off, they notice, and they judge. They pick up whatever evidence becomes available. It is the job of the teacher to ensure that as much favourable evidence as possible is laid out during those thirty or forty minutes.

It might pay you to give some thought to the sort of impression you are creating while you are doing your wonderful, absorbing teaching. How are they processing the evidence that you are laying before them? There are fifteen, twenty, thirty pairs of eyes there, most of them with twenty-twenty vision. Pretty good ears too. Between them, they are going to see or hear *something*.

For example, what do you look like?

I don't mean tall or short, fat or thin, pale or florid, plain or ravishing. There's nothing much you can do about that. We all have to live with our imperfections. So do they, and they know it. If it is a definite disability, they can be remarkably understanding and tolerant. Particularly if it is something they can see. Oddities of behaviour is another matter. They won't understand them, and can be unkind, even cruel.

But that is not on my agenda. I am not an educational psychologist, or any other kind of psychologist, and I am not qualified to offer comment on the topic.

I am talking about things that can be easily observed. In this context, I mean things that can possibly be altered or modified slightly so as to create some kind of improvement, in the cause of better teaching. Things that are within the scope of any teacher.

I have talked elsewhere about the value of being smart. As I said, not a fashion plate or a candidate for 'Best-dressed man'. Just cared-for, healthy, and presentable. There are other matters to consider.

Do your pockets bulge with overfilled wallets and badly-folded letters? Does your brief-case sag half-open with its gaping zip spewing sprawling papers? Can you not do a little pruning? Do you travel light, or do you lug lots of things about with you? Some people have a knack of somehow attracting luggage like burrs from a weed-packed field. When they enter a room, they seem to half-fill it. By the time they have put everything down, every chair and surface is occupied. (Simply going about the place too. It often seems that they're the ones with voluminous, open overcoats, umbrellas, and long face-screening scarves as well.) Ask yourself, do you really need all that clobber for every single class you go into?

If you let this habit get out of hand, they will come to know you as Mr Overgear or Miss Netbag. All it needs is a little thought in advance. If you really do need to carry a great deal for a particular lesson, there is always Pupil Power. It's quite a good way of making an entrance. You can't beat a good entrance (look at Chapter One). You're not weighed down; you are cool and calm, organising and dishing out orders from the word go. Good. Don't let the material get on top of you.

Think about what you will need during the lesson – the tiny things. Are you supplied with the necessary writing tools for both paper and board? Did you renew that worn-out red one? Have you got the right plugs and wires? Have you tested that posh bit of kit beforehand? There's nothing that makes a pupil's eyes go up towards the heavens faster than gadgets that don't work.

Even tinier things: do you have to rummage for a pencil in a huge handbag? Do papers and folders cascade out when you open your book cupboard? Can you put your hand on the right file – at once – when you open the cabinet? Hell, it's your cabinet.

Think for a moment. If you went to a lecture, and some of things I have described happened, what would go through your head?

All these mini-messes are avoidable. You can not hide behind the screen of inexperience.

This is the visual bit: what you look like. Now, what do you sound like? It's important. It would be easy to conclude that, in our present TV-trained, camera-cloned society, the eyes have it. That's how we take in the vast majority of our information. Which is the more vital to a class of pupils? Radio or television?

There's no contest, is there? They always seem to go for the more recent phenomenon. Offer them the choice of a film in black and white or colour; again, no contest. Black and white is the kiss of death. A fossil. A museum piece. Automatically worthless for all practical modern purposes.

However, I suggest that the eyes do not always have it

in education. The ears 'have it' more perhaps than pupils realise. Even in the worst of Covid lockdowns, when so much teaching has been forced into transmission by means of cinema, Skype, DVD, and whatever, the voice is still present. I doubt if one hears much of teaching by means of silent films.

In normal circumstance, what stands before them most of the time is a talking creature, not a projector or a video machine. I said in a previous chapter that, in front of those classes, you have power. Your voice counts. Socrates never wrote a single word. If he had, surely one of his disciples would have mentioned it. No. It was what he *said*, not what he wrote, or drew, or displayed.

Jesus didn't either. No books, no clay tablets, no cart-stage dramas in the market square. All he had was the voice. (Well, perhaps one or two miracles now and then to make a point, but it was mainly the voice, wasn't it?) It makes you wonder what Jesus sounded like. It must have been some voice.

Well, you can't feed thousands with some barley loaves and a few fishes, and it is unlikely that any headmaster will lay on a class of pupils on a convenient hillside to listen to you preach, but it *is* likely that you could improve the way you use your voice in the classroom.

I don't mean an accent. We are not in a *Pygmalion* situation. Nobody would presume to try and teach you to 'tawk proppa'. If you do have an accent, keep it. Treasure it. Be proud of it. It's you. And it is yourself that you are projecting – not John Gielgud.

But – but – I put it to you with all delicacy – is your diction, your delivery, totally unimprovable? Is your normal manner of speech fast or slow? More likely to err on the side of speed, I would say, because most of us can easily become lazy or careless. Consider the process of elision, swallowing syllables, half-words, even whole words. Does 'obviously' come out as 'ovusly'? Instead of 'particular', do they hear 'pticlar'? Do things 'deteriate' instead of 'deteriorate'? Do these criticisms indicate pedantry, or would you tolerate them as excusable human weaknesses? When does speed and urgency become sloppiness? After all, you are a teacher, concerned with teaching respect for learning, and that includes, presumably, care for your own language. If the world can't expect an example from its teachers, where do they look?

Now consider this. How do you flow? Can you get through a couple of sentences without, as they say in the game, hesitation, irrelevance, or repetition? If you are in the trade of words – and you are – you ought to be better at it than most. All of us have some little tics and habits of speech; most of us do not often have to string several sentences together all at one go, as it were. Teachers have to string sentences together all the time. So, if you are inclined to say 'er – ' or 'um – ' or 'OK' or 'now then' or 'right!', it will show up in larger numbers. That's when they begin to count them up and compare with the previous lesson.

One of the worst 'offences' is, I suppose, 'kind of', or 'like', or – the mortal sin – 'kindoflike'. I'm sure you are acquainted with plenty more – maybe even guilty of plenty more. Don't worry: reading these pages is as safe as the confessional.

Again, do you know, however roughly, what you are going to say when you open your mouth? Do you know where your sentence is going? Do you regularly have to correct yourself, change tack, even go on as if the previous three phrases have been deleted.

Politicians are supposed to be even better at speaking than teachers, but just listen to them sometimes. I once tuned in to an experienced foreign secretary answering a journalist's question. He stopped, corrected himself, and went back to the beginning *six times*. At the end of that charade, he still had not addressed the question. This was not the customary politician's trick of doing anything but provide an answer; when they do that, they can hardly stop talking. No. This man simply didn't know what he was going to say and kept changing his mind. Just what were his mental processes? And in charge of the nation's foreign fortunes.

The great Anglo-American journalist Alistair Cooke called the process 'muddy thinking'. He followed it up by saying that it proceeded from a muddy mind. Well, of course, we don't want our teachers to have muddy minds, do we?

Simpler still: can they hear you? Do you speak with your head up? Not like the Grenadier Guards, obviously (or 'ovusly'), but high enough. Are you clear? Do they have to strain?

I once had an English teacher whose lungs had been damaged by gas, and the result was that his voice barely rose above a whisper. Well, that's what it seemed like. He was a remarkable man; he turned his disability into an advantage. He had a shock of white hair, a formidable bristling white moustache, an unfailingly smart, waistcoated suit, a very military bearing, and a pair of commanding eyes. I was not the only boy there who was physically afraid of him. Because his voice was so faint, we used to strain to catch what he said, because we dared not miss anything. His class control was like iron. It is not necessarily an example I would recommend, but he was a good instance of making the best of what you've got.

Do you project your voice? Teaching is not the same as talking. You don't have to shout, but, as I have said before – probably more than once – a lesson is not a chat. I have no idea what goes on in an actor's training academy, but I would venture to guess that some attention is given to the projection of the voice. How else can they get students to make a stage whisper heard in the gallery? One might wonder how much attention is given today in teacher training colleges to the projection of the voice.

And, while we're on the subject, how much attention is given there, not to the projection of the voice but to the *protection* of it. A stage actor in a leading role is working for, at most, a couple of hours of an evening. A film actor can often spend three-quarters of the day waiting for the sun to come out. A teacher with an eight-period day is using his voice rather more than that, especially if you add on a lunch-hour dinner duty, an hour of football coaching after school, and a parents' evening. Any teacher will tell you that the commonest complaint is a sore throat. I wonder if any medical research has been done about complaints and diseases of the throat among teachers.

How do you look? What do they think of what they see? Can they hear you? Now think of the teacher's dreaded weapon – the red pen. Can they read you?

They have done their homework. You have done yours, and given back the exercise books on time. What do your margin comments look like? Dense? Microscopic? Faded because that biro is running out again? Alternatively, is their own text cringing beneath the onslaught of erasions, underlinings (double, triple), and exclamation marks? Even (not unknown) wrong spellings? I remember seeing one Chemistry teacher's report to the effect that: 'His spelling is disasterous.'

If a teacher is hard pressed, and he sees yet another repetition of a common mistake, after he has laboured the point *ad nauseam* (his *nauseam*, not theirs), one can understand why he might use the pen as a scimitar and leave a mighty red gash right across the page. It will have relieved his feelings, but it won't have done much for those of the pupil.

As a matter of fact, you can improve your handwriting. I don't mean mount a copperplate campaign with the inkpot and the quill pen, and perch on a high stool to give a dash of atmosphere. No time for that; there's some teaching to be done. But, if, when you look closely, you notice that you regularly murder a particular letter, you can, with some concentration and persistence, get to the stage whereat you will write the 'new' letter without thinking. It's not difficult.

I was once reading a note written by an elderly aunt, and was very taken by the way she formed a particular capital letter. I hadn't seen one like it before. I thought, 'I'd like one like that.' So I worked at it. Honestly, it didn't take very long. All right, it was a youthful affectation, but my point is that, in well under a month, I could do capital T's just like Auntie Florrie's – without thinking.

Finally, if they *can* read you, what do they read? Do you offer anything besides ticks and crosses? Anyone can correct an exercise. Marking it is a different matter. At the risk of sounding pious, it helps if you can take the opportunity (if it presents itself) to indicate something they have done right as well as something they have done wrong.

A touch of humour helps too. I found the chance for that in a boy's 'A' Level History essay. He had taken a mighty long time to get going; he was not on top of his material. He was not quite sure how to go about presenting it all. Like a good essayist, he wrote an introduction all right. The trouble was that, after he had done that, he wasn't satisfied, and proceeded to write another one. And another. He was near the bottom of the page before he actually got around to answering the question. So at this point, in the margin, I simply wrote 'Ah!'

I watched him as I handed it back. When he read down to the crunch, he laughed out loud and said, 'Ah! Essay starts here.' He'd got it. And I hadn't had to criticise. It doesn't often work out as neatly as that.

Self-improvement, we all know, is supposed to be good for the soul. But we also know that a teacher is not expected to devote regular hours to breast-beating and self-examination. Moderation in all things. Life and the working day are too short. He has a job to do. And pupils are generally happiest if he gets on and does it. One can be too earnest.

But try and keep one tiny antenna out, to pick up any vibes that happen to be around.

13 A good story

Ask anyone to give you their views on education and stand by for a ready answer. I doubt if many people would make a wry face and say, 'Me? Oh, I'm no expert.'

Why? Because everybody *is* an expert on education. Why again? Because everybody has been to school. From five to sixteen. If you have eleven years' experience of something under your belt, you feel in a good position to hold forth about it. If you have suffered it, you know about it. Of course the depth and breadth of that knowledge can vary wildly.

What comes out can be anything from partisan pontification about poverty and privilege, right down to the fierce assertion that 'when we were at school, we had to mind'.

Well, yes, we have all heard the law being laid down along those lines, and we give these fervent observations the attention they deserve. But try timing your question to catch them in a more quiet, thoughtful mood, and ask, 'What do you think, then, are the elements vital to good teaching?'

With luck, you should get a more considered answer. Most people think that their children should be educated efficiently, to however modest a degree. You will, I hope, hear references to things like discipline, purpose, planning, knowledge, example, humanity, a broad curriculum. Any of our 'experts' could add to that little catalogue, and he would probably be right. Nobody, however, is likely to produce a universally acceptable comprehensive list. If he were to show signs of doing so, you might checkmate him with the suggestion that no list would be complete till you have added stories.

Stories are the dream recipe for a gap in the educational market.

One of the first, and most frustrating, things a pupil discovers is that he or she forgets things. If that isn't a gap in the market, I don't know what is. If someone could come up with a recipe for keeping everything we are told in the memory – and easily retrievable – he would deserve the Nobel Prize, and every pupil would be happy to contribute to the cost of it (which I understand is quite considerable).

Put the other way round, a lot of things we meet at school can be difficult, but there is one that is dead easy – forgetting what Sir said five minutes ago. That Latin teacher I talked about in a previous chapter observed one day that it was easier to learn Science than it was to learn Latin and Greek. An example? Well, take the radio, he said. Anyone could explain how a radio worked in less than half an hour.

At the end of one term, Bunter did just that. He explained how a radio worked. I actually understood. And it didn't seem all that difficult. What a super little packet of general knowledge to have safe in one's pocket, so to speak. What happened? By the end of the lunch-hour I had forgotten a good deal of it. By the end of the week it had gone. Completely. Not a clue left.

That's where stories come in. They help us to remember. They are not the cure-all for treacherous memories, naturally, and I do not know offhand of a story which would help us to remember how a radio works. Nevertheless, I claim that the point is valid. In many circumstances, stories can be a mighty big help. Why? Because they add so many extra ingredients to the lesson – drama, suspense, humour, character, all sorts of things.

How do you make things stick? With glue. And a story is the glue which sticks things to the memory. Unlike the rest of education, you don't have to sell it; all you have to do is tell it.

You're on safe ground; everyone likes stories. They are not just a little treat to end the primary school day. They are not a modern little trick thought up to make school life palatable. As far back as our historical memories can go, men, women, and children have sat round fires and listened to stories. They knew how important stories were. When books became common, and even more so when the printing press got to work, there were many misgivings, because it was felt that it would make people solitary, and so spoil, even destroy, the atmosphere of sharing and togetherness round the camp fire. Similar fears are voiced today about the influence of computer games on the social life of children.

Stories have a vast fund of virtues, a fathomless lineage, and an impeccable pedigree. Uniquely, they have an equal appeal to both seller and buyer; telling them is as much fun as listening to them.

Stories, however brief, can instantly change instruction into entertainment. They are the perfect classroom anaesthetic; they can help to make learning painless. Or, if not painless, at least more bearable. Hardly surprising that Jesus thought they were a good idea. If they could help to get popular theology across to illiterate crowds in the open air, they are in with a good chance in the comparative peace and comfort of the classroom.

I'm sorry if you think I have laboured the point, but it is

an important one. Not at the expense of other points, no, but simply important in its own right. But it is so ordinary, and so obvious (like many other things in education), that it can be easily underestimated, even overlooked.

If you want the edifice of your teaching technique to look good, the small features of it need as much care as the big ones. The concert pianist makes the little twiddly bits in his concerto look as easy and impressive as the mighty double octave crescendos. The same with teaching; everything counts. Detail. Detail. Detail.

Even the little tricks you toss aside, which you appear to throw away. They have to be just as good. Pupils are great scavengers, and pick up all sorts of bits and pieces which you may have forgotten about. Once you begin to get a little crafty, you can tailor these little scraps, and you learn when and where to toss them on to their path. One of Bunter's which I fastened on to was: 'The trouble in the world is that it's the evil people who are so dashed energetic.' (His word – 'dashed'.)

Even then you will get surprises. A forty-year-old will come up to you and remind of you of something you said years ago which had impressed him – a comment, an observation, a little incident you recalled for them. And you had forgotten all about it.

You never know just how much is going in. Keep at it. It's often more than you think.

I had a favourite story that I used to tell, about a ghost at Stonehenge – you know, huge, forbidding stones, dark night, howling wind, horrible faces. If it was possible, I would tell it in an afternoon period on a dark and stormy day in December. Turn the lights out, of course. It had a wonderful punch line too. Quite a scarer. It really got in amongst them.

One morning long, long after, I was having a cup of coffee in a local hotel. The lady who served me looked familiar, but I couldn't place her exactly. When she brought me the bill, she reminded me of that ghost at Stonehenge. She had remembered it for over thirty years.

That's all very well, you may say. But we can't all be Hans Christian Andersen or Scheherazade. Neither can I. I couldn't have thought up *The Little Mermaid* or *Ali Baba and the Forty Thieves* in a hundred years.

Never fear; you don't have to *create* these stories. If you could, you might stand a chance of making a good deal more money than you would in front of a class. All you have to do is t*ell* them. You can find them anywhere, from cruising the internet to listening in the back seat of a number 27 bus.

However, telling them, though straightforward, does still present its problems. You may not have to think them up, but you do have to dress them up.

For a start, you are not writing; you are talking. The two are not the same. There is a great deal they can get from the printed page, true. And if you have been able to get through to the subconscious, you will get across more than the printed words actually say.

It can happen that you have a particular remembrance of a story – say, a random action, a momentary flash of behaviour. Years later, you may still recall it vividly, and, out of fondness, turn to the book to find again where it actually occurred – and it's not there. The writer did his job so well that he put that thought in your mind, and you were the one who put it on the page, not him.

There is a great deal too that they can get from the

recited page, as any parent knows who has told the compulsory bedtime story – even if he tells the same one several times. And Heaven help him if he gets a detail wrong.

No. I am concerned with the spoken story, which just appears to 'come out'. It doesn't, of course. In a good lesson, most things don't just 'happen'; teachers make them happen. How? Tricks of the trade.

Making something look spontaneous is one of the most difficult tricks of all. The concert pianist who is playing a world-famous sonata for the thousandth time, and making you feel that you're hearing it for the *first* time. The actor who nearly drops a bar of wet soap in a matinee performance of a long run, and he can make it look as if it was an accident.

Spontaneity is a winner, but my word, it takes a lot of work to get it to go wrong 'right'. Before you can do that, you have to be absolutely sure that you can do it right 'right'. Tommy Cooper, as I said, was a compulsive rehearser for his act in which the tricks *nearly* went wrong.

So with telling a story. *Voilà!* In the middle of a lesson. With no book and no prompting. It just comes. If it is done well, what goes in is not only the factual detail of the story, but the spirit of it – the subconscious bit.

I was on a bus from Hastings to the town of Battle, on my way to look at the site of the Battle of Hastings. It was fairly empty (the bus), and the conductor was happy to have a gossip. I explained the purpose of my journey. He replied that he had always enjoyed his History lessons at school. He singled out Ancient Rome as the particular object of his fondness.

He inclined his head in token of admiration.

'Ah,' he said. 'Them Romans.'

I would put money on the fact that one of his teachers had told him a story or two, quite likely in primary school. What that teacher had succeeded in doing was more than making him acquainted with the Romans. He had conveyed awe at their achievement, and his pupil had caught it. And caught it securely enough to pass it to a passenger in his bus thirty years later. You don't do that just by compiling a set of notes and setting a revision test. Stories were in there somewhere. Somewhere along the line he had had a good teacher, and that teacher had taken the trouble to learn a little about the technique of telling them.

Telling stories is great fun, but it is sensible to put your enjoyment second. What comes first is the impact on your audience. They have to 'get it'. Nothing must come in the way. All padding goes; remember you have only a few minutes in the middle of a lesson. Keep the language simple, direct. It must all go one way – forward to the *dénouement*. So it must have pace; they have to know it is going somewhere. Get your order of events tight and logical. If you can put in some suspense, so much the better. Drop a hint here and there. This is another reason why you need to prepare. The kiss of death for a story is: 'Oh, I forgot to tell you that… ' It must all sound simple, but they mustn't know how hard you have worked to make everything come in the right order, in the right strength, at the right speed.

Don't be afraid to add touches of your own. I don't mean change anything. It is well known that the truth should never be allowed to get in the way of a good story, but you must keep the spirit of the truth. What you put in of your own should be enhancements, not corruptions. For example, in the famous story of the Wooden Horse of Troy, which as you know was the brain child of Odysseus, the Wily One of the Greek princes, I have Odysseus suggesting that the Greeks send out a patrol to measure the width of the main gateway of the city. This was so that the Greek engineers could deliberately make the chassis of the trolley on which the great horse stood too wide, so that the Trojans would have to dismantle part of the city gateway to allow it to pass.

You haven't bent the story; you have sharpened it just a little. A young audience can savour a touch of low cunning like that. The more often you tell the story, the more such similar touches will occur to you. Don't get too bemused with your own cleverness; the story must still move. Even so, you can get a few happy little inspirations. But only a few.

There must be no surplus flesh on it. Listen to Tommy Cooper's jokes or to his setting the scene for one of his tricks. Not a syllable is wasted.

Incidentally, I usually called Odysseus Ulysses, which is technically wrong. 'Ulysses' is the Latin version. 'Odysseus' is the correct Greek one. But I have always found that 'Odysseus' presents much bigger problems of spelling than 'Ulysses'. After all, you want them to get it all down on paper for homework without any agony, don't you? Don't put avoidable obstacles in the way. 'Ulysses' is hard enough.

Well, that's what I did. I never ceased to marvel how much they were bowled over by the whole Trojan epic – Helen, Paris, the elopement, the gathering of the 'thousand ships', the siege, Achilles, Hector, the gods, the whole show. This story is over 3,000 years old, and it used to slay them every time. Just stand back and let them get stuck in. I always got the best homeworks of the year out of it.

Once again, you may feel daunted by all this. 'I'll never manage all that. All those subtleties. All that drama. I'll never be able to keep that up for so long.'

All right. If you can't tell long stories, tell short ones. Anecdotes. They can be just as effective and memorable. The shortest one I know is:

'Hired.

'Tired?

'Fired!'

Yes, pretty corny. I'm sure you can manage something better than that. But because you have so little 'ammunition' to play with, every tiny content has to count. Every squib has to fire.

The great attraction of them is that they are so manageable, so do-able.

Because they are short, they don't tax the memory. You can polish them, hone them, practise them. They can always be sharpened. The tiniest inflection of the voice can make the difference between a pat and a punch.

Once you have these little gems under control, you can trot them out at any time. Often, the more 'throw-away' they are, the greater their impact. Keep at them. Pare them, trim them. The barer they are, like the undulating stripteaser, the more attention they will get. Remember always to ration them. Trump cards are by definition in a minority. As always, moderation.

Another advantage is that they are so easily remembered, and, if they're good, quoted. Get yourself quoted, and your profile begins to rise (we hope, for the right reasons).

Anecdotes like these are a good illustration of the old saw that 'brevity is the soul of wit'. They can have not only wit but bite. And memorability. It can be amazing how much quite scholarly stuff can stick with the most ordinary of pupils.

Another of my favourite story subjects was the great general of Carthage, Hannibal. That's right – he of the elephants. I was shopping in the timber department of a local store when the supervisor reminded me of some lessons I had done with his class on ancient history. 'Oh, yes,' he said, 'the Punic Wars'. Now, ancient history may be a part of a working man's general knowledge. Hannibal too, because of his elephants. But the Punic Wars are not. You could ask a hundred people in the street about the Punic Wars, and be met with blank faces. But this man had grasped it, and held it for years. The power of stories.

It may be argued that I was lucky teaching History, because it was stiff with stories. But surely any practitioner in any other subject can come up with anecdotes from his own specialism. Every subject has its own anthology. At the most elementary level, think of apples in Physics, and in RE too if it comes to that. Veritable snowdrifts of them in English and Foreign Literature.

Anywhere else for that matter. A correspondence column, the playground, the public bar. Stories can refresh the driest of lessons. They can be found growing everywhere. They are there, waiting to be spotted, picked, preserved, shaped, shared, and savoured.

14 The debate on leadership

When you begin work on anything in which a lot of people are involved, at once you are somewhere on a scale. It might be right at the bottom; it might be right at the top. The lowest form of animal life or the Lord High Executioner. The most likely status you will have will put you somewhere in between.

That means that there will be people above you – bigger, tougher, smarter, richer, more experienced, or, most likely, with more stripes on their sleeve. You will have to learn how to deal with them. I am concerned in this chapter with those at the other end – those below you. There will be times when you want to get them to do things because you have said so. How are you going to manage that?

Most obviously, as I said, it will be because of the stripes on your own sleeve. That makes them obedient. Ideally, of course, you would like them to be willing as well, but that involves something else. As a general rule, it is called leadership.

A cloud of, for want of a better word, 'significance' has been allowed to gather round the concept of leadership. Other words which imply similar authority have not been so invested. We don't hear much about officership, prime-minister-ship, bossmanship, or chairmanship. Perhaps it is because 'leadership' suggests an element of bravado, *élan*, charisma – a touch of magic which is beyond the reach, never mind the grasp, of humble mortals like ourselves. By implication there is in the mix a dash of Alexander the Great, Robin Hood, and Robert E. Lee. We can't be like them, can we? But that does not prevent a host of 'experts' telling us, at great length, how to become leaders – in the boardroom, on the podium, the field of play, the factory floor, the field of battle. Everywhere. Including the classroom. All with their own codes and formulas and vocabulary and recipes for success – their own 'system'.

This talk is ubiquitous. So is the literature. In teacher training too.

You, the willing but tentative beginner, can be forgiven for concluding that there is a mighty mystique obscuring it. Nothing is actually spelt out, but so much attention is devoted to leadership talk that the implication is unmistakable: it is of absolutely cosmic importance, and it demands gifts and qualities of transcendental virtue. That poor student – you – may well wonder, and who could blame you, whether you are, frankly, up to it.

You are, rest assured. I have no idea what percentage of the young adult population want to become teachers, but I would hazard a guess that it is pretty low. So, economically speaking, you are valuable. From the word go. You are quite rare birds.

As for wondering if you've got what it takes, anyone who wants to spend his or her future working days standing in front of a group of young people, trying to help them to enjoy a more abundant life, is a potential leader already. No matter how hesitant he may feel.

It is no sin to be daunted. It is a great virtue to be willing to go ahead in spite of *being* daunted. You are much better equipped to become a successful teacher than the clever cock who thinks it's going to be a piece of cake, and who has his career moves mapped out in order to make it to a headship in a dozen years. Got his boxes all ready to tick when the time comes. God help his future pupils, and God help his future staff.

If you are daunted, that means you wish you knew more, and are willing to learn more. A promising start.

Everyone can learn. Just as every new mother and every new father can learn about becoming a parent. And they, poor souls, haven't even passed an exam for it. It doesn't stop them. It shouldn't stop you.

It is all too easy to think of shining examples when you contemplate any activity. The next step is to worry that you won't reach up to their lofty standards and achievements. The young officer may feel that he doesn't have it to be a field marshal; the young priest knows in his heart that he is not archbishop material, the young engineer accepts that he is unlikely to become the inventor of a new war machine. But those professions are not chock full of conquerors and saintly primates and creators of bouncing bombs. Most of us are ordinary. Don't be overawed by the brilliant few.

There is still scope everywhere, all the time, to be a good officer or a good priest or a good engineer. The same with teaching; there is scope to be a leader too, even if you don't understand a word of the jargon in the leadership books.

I have never been impressed by the ball-of-fire advisers and inspectors who descend on a class and proceed to give a brilliant performance in a 'show' lesson. Dazzling. Everyone agrees. Perhaps even the pupils too.

But that's one lesson – no doubt rehearsed and honed and polished and trotted out in a procession of carefully-selected classroom situations around the county, in an atmosphere which is bound to be a mite artificial, to say the least.

But let him try doing it with form 2C or 5Z, three, four, five times a week, for thirty-five weeks – with the homework and the marking and chasing of laggards and listening to the excuses, and all the rest. That's where the teaching is done. In the galleys, day by day.

This idea could go back to something I said in the first chapter about 'Teaching small'. Teaching is not about prodigies; it is about detail, scraps, bits and pieces, dotting i's and crossing t's. Easily overlooked in the ranking, but there all the time. It is not dinosaurs which build the great white cliffs; it is the millions of microscopic molluscs. Teaching is a profession of routine and humdrummery. There are tiny things around you all the time, which give you the chance – maybe not to be Joan of Arc or George Washington – but to make a pupil slightly more willing to have a go than he was yesterday. That is realistic; you can do that, and you know you can.

If there is an open space near the school which is not big enough for a football field, and there is no money for a basketball court, don't think of it as an eyesore. Try instead to imagine a space for a biological field study, a homemade observatory, a weather station. I may be open to criticism for the actual choice of projects, but I think my point is still sound; if you notice a need or an opportunity, and you offer, inspire, and create a way of filling that need, or turning that opportunity into achievement, you are leading. You won't need the books; your own enthusiasm will carry you along and tell you what to do.

If, having studied the curriculum, and being aware of a particular skill you have that is unique to yourself, you are able to offer a course of lessons – don't even call them lessons; just 'sessions' of something or other – that will appeal to pupils who are not bewitched by the usual attractions on offer, you are leading.

I had a colleague who taught Maths – not the most hypnotic of subjects. He was a nice fellow, a good colleague, but, to look at him, he did not ooze adventure. He did not play football, hockey, rugby, or cricket. But he did like table-tennis. And he set about introducing table-tennis into a rather conservative school with a strong tradition of hockey and cricket and rowing, and who habitually referred to table-tennis as 'ping-pong'. That gives you an idea of what he was up against.

Starting with a few enthusiasts, a solitary table which had to be folded up and put away every night, and to the accompaniment of a good deal of leg-pull, he built a thriving club, with several school teams and a presence in local leagues which went well beyond the usual inter-school rivalry.

He had capitalised on his own passion, spotted a potential gap, worked hard, and built an enviable organ-isation which the partisans of other more conventional sports had to recognise and respect. That was leadership. They couldn't have done it without him.

You can display leadership anywhere; you don't even have to go outside the classroom. There is no need to cross the Antarctic or trundle elephants over the Alps.

Every teacher has a willing pupil who is struggling, and struggling not because of lack of effort or lack of ability but because of lack of confidence. There was one girl I remember who had trouble making the transition from 'GCSE' work to 'A' Level. If it's clearer, from year 11 to year 12. There's a gear change, isn't there? 'GCSE' tries to find out if you have a memory; 'A' Level sets out to discover whether you have a mind.

This girl, like thousands of others before her, did not make the transition easily. Once again, think small. I would pick out a promising sentence or two. I didn't just put a 'G' in the margin; I tried to explain *why* it was good, and compared it with some of her others.

Then we moved on. I can actually remember handing one essay back to her and saying, 'Look at that paragraph. Now, *that* is History. [I would try to explain why.] You have written something historical. What we have to aim for next time is to write not one historical paragraph but two or three, and then two or three all strung together. And then of course, in time, the whole essay. Get the idea?'

She did. We had opened a door, and she knew where to go when she got inside. You could see her whole demeanour blossom. No, she didn't get an 'A' star, but she got a very respectable 'B'. And went on to hold down a prestigious job at the V. and A. Museum. Was that all me? No, of course it wasn't. But I helped. Very often it is not so much the leg up itself as the timing of it. I was lucky; I happened to say it at the right moment. But I am pleased enough with myself to record it in my credit ledger.

Among other qualities of leadership is the trick of showing them that something or other is do-able. You don't have to be Captain Scott or Hannibal to do that.

How about this? You can turn negative situations into positive ones, though it is perhaps a little more chancy. Once again, every teacher has had, or has, a pupil who is bright, promising, even talented – but idle. Or maybe just going through a bad patch. A broken heart is a common culprit. Well, it's painful, isn't it? Especially the first time.

Whatever the cause, and whatever the symptoms, you don't need the advice columns or the text books to tell you that what the patient needs is a shock, a ticking off, a kick in the pants. You should be able to do that all right. You may even be able to remember when a perceptive teacher did the same to you. OK, but gauge it carefully; there are kicks and kicks.

As always, it is a question of balance. You have to know how hard to hit, where, and when. But, if you have built a good relationship, they will know that you are on their side, and they will take it. If they don't, then either you have over-estimated your 'pull' over them (a human enough error) or they are too far gone for you to be of any assistance in that way. You can't win them all.

There must be countless other similar situations, some of which you have heard about, some within your own experience. I have probably laboured the point long enough to show that each of them offers an opportunity to display leadership of one kind or another. It doesn't have to be prodigious. Time and again, people remember small things about you.

You can labour through the midnight oil to prepare the brilliant lesson, brim full of timely advice, succinct comments, penetrating observations, searching questions, brilliant revelations, and magical moments (you think), and it will all go right past them. They don't say it was good and they don't say it was bad. *They don't say anything at all* – that's much worse. And fifteen years later someone leading a couple of toddlers by the hand will come up and remind you of a remark which had never ceased to impress them, and you have forgotten you even said it. Well, take heart: at least you said *something* memorable.

It's a funny old game, to be sure.

Take heart too from this very paradox. Doing the small things, I mean. They often reflect the principles and values that you consider important. Because they run so deep, you tend not to be conscious of them, but whenever you practise them, they reflect you. It's another paradox that we make less impression when we try hard, and more when we are unself-conscious. And of course the impression is more genuine.

If you write neatly, or mark carefully, they see it. If you polish your shoes, they observe it. If you pay attention to detail, they appreciate that you have noticed. Particularly if it is an individual. You have noticed *them*. *They* matter. It all adds up.

I was once in the cast of a school Christmas play. The producer was a fierce Chemistry teacher whose eyes scared the life out of us. 'A.D.' we called him. Those were the initials of his Christian names. After it was all over, I received a handwritten letter thanking me for the part I had played in the production. I wasn't very good, but the letter recognised that it was a team effort. A.D. was a man of immense presence and authority, and *he had written to me, in person, man to man*. (And presumably everyone else.) I still have that letter.

In each case you are setting some kind of example. They can see you doing it, and it looks as if it is well within their scope. It's the easiest leadership technique of all – example. You don't have to work at it; it's you. If they think it is worth doing, they will follow. Presto – you are a leader.

It is a truism, I believe, that a team or an orchestra, or any group, will absorb some of the style and character of its coach, or its conductor, or its manager. All unconscious. But the leadership is going on.

Always remember that though pupils can be all sorts of things – difficult, unpredictable, volatile, fickle, awkward, plain bolshy, and at times merciless – they are also young. They haven't been alive very long. They don't know very much. They haven't had enough time. They don't know what's out there. Of course they want to be told; they want to be shown; they want to be led. And there you are with a golden opportunity. You won't get a more needy audience, though they won't admit it. (They're tough, remember? They know everything, and they have a built-in suspicion of anything which is reckoned to be good for them.)

Oh – and even if you succeed, don't expect them always to turn round and say thank you. You may have to wait twenty years for that, but they can turn a moving compliment when the time comes and they are so disposed. Ask any mature teacher you respect and he will give you an example.

I've said this before and I shall no doubt say it again. So much of the teaching business, and the leadership business too, is simple, though not always easy. It helps if you don't arrive on the job with too many settled attitudes, preconceived ideas, over-ambitious aspirations. Just come to the work, give it the once-over, and trust yourself to tease out something commonsensical which needs to be done – and which is within your scope to do.

Sometimes, you will find, to your surprise, that it is both simple *and* easy. Forget the experts. To hell with the mystique. Stop *trying* to be a leader. Just look and think. Or, as Sherlock Holmes would say, 'Don't just look; observe.'

So much of leadership, really, springs from good sense, common decency, human kindness, and native wit. It may not always be easy to do, but it is usually easy to see when it needs to be done. Well, you're part of the way there already.

You often hear it said that 'old Mr. So-and-so', our dear old English teacher, wouldn't have survived in the classrooms of today. Everything was now too fast, too tough, too brash, too everything. What they forget is that the much-revered, well-wrinkled veterans of today were the young lions of yesterday. What did they do? They arrived, sized up the situation, and evolved a technique to deal with the problems and personalities it had thrown up. They listened, they observed, and they learned. And they got on with it.

My two sports masters were like that. By the time I met them they were well established, at the height of their powers. They had done what they thought was necessary. They didn't have a rule book. They didn't bounce around in track suits. They did not hobnob and hug and pat on the back. The hockey master was rarely seen even to pick up a hockey stick. The cricket master did not raise his voice above a leisurely drawl. And our respect for them was profound.

How did they do it? Perhaps there is a touch of mystery after all.

15 Classroom bureaucracy

I READ SOMEWHERE ONCE that for every fully-trained and -equipped soldier in the front line there are twenty-seven other people whose job contributes to putting him there and keeping him there.

In a roundabout sort of way, the same thing applies to teaching. By the time you stand at your desk and open your notes and ask them to get out their books, a lot has been going on elsewhere. It's not like the 'old-fashioned tango, where there's nothing to it; you just sort of stand there and just sort of do it'.

Nobody should 'sort of' do teaching, any more than anybody should 'sort of' do brain surgery.

So much for the sermon. Now, the practice.

I do not necessarily claim that it takes as many as twenty-seven other people to put a teacher in front of a class. Whatever the real number is, it is unarguable, though, that a lot of decisions have been taken before you walk into that classroom.

Most of them are out of your range, quite often beyond your power, some even beyond your knowledge. You have to accept living with the results of them: school layout, size of class, length of lessons, budgets, school catchment area, fresh government legislation, school implementation of that legislation, length of lunch-hour, a thousand things right down to the regulations for fire alarm practice. The new teacher's head spins when all the rules are trotted out at the pre-term staff briefing. He can, initially, feel almost as baffled as the new pupil who wonders whether he can remember where the toilets are.

At least you have something in common with the

pupils: you are both lumping it to a considerable extent. Nearly all the things you have to accept they have to accept too. And probably many more. I suppose the most basic one is the human factor: you don't get to choose your classes, and they certainly don't have any choice with their teachers. The young are experts at lumping it. Just think of all the things, both in and out of school, that they have to 'lump'. (See Chapter 11.)

Maybe one exception for a teacher: if you are a head of department, you do have some control over which classes you teach, but your professional integrity dictates, doesn't it, that you give yourself a strong slice of the difficult ones, and you make sure that your young probationer is not thrown to the wolves of 4Q, who eat beginners for breakfast.

Nevertheless, notwithstanding, and be that as it may, you can still find ways and means by which you can make your working life just a little more manageable. If you like, you still have scope for creating, even extending, your own comfort zone.

As with so many of the topics I refer to, some of what I am about to say may appear so elementary and obvious that perhaps I should offer an apology for mentioning it. But here we go anyway.

Consider doors. Some teachers believe that the atmosphere a teacher creates is essentially a private one. So doors should be shut. Some teachers again take this a little further; they don't like any other adult in the room while they are teaching. Inspectors, advisers, VIP's are tolerated as a necessary evil, like a routine trip to the dentist. But certainly not parents. Nor casual visitors perambulating up the passage and poking their heads round the door.

Other teachers don't mind. Some people just like open doors; others like shut ones. Perhaps it's something deeply psychological, I don't know. For instance, when I am writing, I don't like having the door gaping wide. I am not compiling state secret dossiers for MI5; I just prefer the door more shut than open.

Readers of this may wonder what all the fuss is about: for Heaven's sake, just shut the damn door or leave it open, and get started. I simply wanted to make the point that you usually have an option, and you may have legitimate reasons for one or the other. It is a tiny freedom that is usually available to you.

It's not the same with windows. It is most unlikely that any 'expert' who doubted the value of fresh air would attract many followers, and I have not met the teacher who would agree with him. Think: twenty or thirty bodies in an enclosed space, either on a summer afternoon or with the pipes full on in November, many of them sweating after a lunch-hour's playground football. There really is no argument.

But some windows stay shut. Why? Because teachers forget. They have a hundred tiny thoughts about the previous lesson jostling in their minds with another hundred about the lesson they are about to start. Minds have limits.

I was lucky; I had a memorable reminder early in my first year's teaching. My headmaster had a rich command of pithy remarks which could fit a situation like a glove. One afternoon he came into my class for some routine business or other. He conducted it, paused, looked round the room (luckily their heads were down), and whispered conspiratorially to me, 'It smells rather of hot boy in here.'

I leapt to do his unspoken bidding. He had conveyed neglect and urgency without inducing in a young teacher any sense of inadequacy. It may not have been good teaching from me, but it was good headmastering from him. And it stuck.

In a sentence then, glance at the windows when you walk in.

So much for the doors and the windows. In the average classroom, there is also an awful lot of wall. Can you do anything about that? Do you *want* to do anything about that?

If it is not your room – just one you spend only a couple of periods in on Monday and Wednesday mornings – there is not much that can be done; it's not your room. But if it is, or at any rate is generally accepted as 'your' room, there is quite a lot.

In fact, a lot of widespread advice suggests, and suggests very strongly, that you not only could be doing it; you *should* be doing it. The accepted gospel according to pictures, posters, and charts.com, is that no wall is properly furnished unless it is plastered with plans, graphs, panoramas, pupils' art projects, progress charts of collections for the latest charity, adverts, calendars, reminders, and I don't know what.

These are in such profusion, and basking in the glow of so many unarguable good reasons, that any mildly dissentient voice could be construed by the purists as bad form, bad taste, bad manners, and bad teaching practice. It would be almost like saying that you disapproved of Christmas cards.

All I wish to do, before I am submerged beneath the surging tide of disapproval from an army of advisers, is to offer one idea – that of balance. The Greeks, who were no slouches in the matter of knowledge, teaching, and learning, had tumbled to that over two and a half thousand years ago. Their motto was 'nothing too much'. Which was very honest of them; they knew they had a strong propensity for going over the top.

As my best Maths teacher, Joe Ellis, used to say, when he stood in front of a problem of geometry or a tricky algebraic formula that he was about to explain, 'Consider.' Look at that wall. Look at what's on it. In a score of different sizes, styles, and colours. Put up by a score of different hands. With a score of different fastenings. At a score of different times. For a score of different reasons depending upon a score of varying priorities.

'Consider,' said Joe. (That was his nickname – 'Joe'. His Headmaster came from Lancashire, where, I was told, everybody called 'Ellis' was promptly nicknamed 'Joe'. Like 'Dusty' with 'Miller or 'Spud' with 'Murphy'.)

What is the point of putting any kind of notice on a wall? Exactly – information. Telling people something, or showing them something. Fine. Splendid. Very virtuous of you. But there is a limit. People, to coin a phrase, are human. They can take in just so much information. Give them a little; they show willing. Give them a lot, and they switch off. Put another way, when do watchable notices become clutter?

That's one point – overcrowding. Another is age – how long has the thing been up there? The more you see tears, folds, curled-up corners, and yellowing paper (even perhaps graffiti), the greater the decline in the significance graph (except, in the case of graffiti, a possible rise in entertainment value). If it is not maintained, how long does it take for a chunk of that wall to become a non-event? And a scruffy wall speaks of neglect, like dirty shoes. What sort of impression are you giving?

To paraphrase our Greek philosophers, it is a question of balance. Of course a wall has its uses; some of them can be vital. But if you want it to perform its intended functions efficiently, as with a motor car or a garden, you have to look after it. A good wall, like a well-maintained car or garden, reflects credit on its custodian. This time the freedom, the option, is very much yours. It is, in effect, up to you to ensure that that wall is more than something you absently gaze at as a better alternative to listening to a boring lesson.

That takes care of the structure. Well, nearly all of it. Keep the floor tidy, obviously. It just looks better. Anything that looks tidier must be a good thing. It speaks control, self-respect, awareness. All tiny things, maybe, but I have said many times already that much of teaching is to do with tiny things. They all count. And it makes an impression that's unconscious. What you are after is control that they accept without thinking.

You don't have to issue half a dozen dustpans and brushes – that's the short cut to chaos, labels you as an eccentric, and is a bad start to a lesson. But ask everybody to bend down and pick up three pieces of litter round their desk, and send someone round with a shoebox to collect it. Only one person moves. That takes about thirty seconds. You have shown that you have standards, initiative, control, resource, and grip. Perhaps a sense of humour too. Not a bad dividend for thirty seconds' delay.

What do we have left? Oh yes – the ceiling. Not much you can do there. Though I did once hear of a teacher who, it was claimed, piled all the furniture so that he could climb up and write, in large letters, on the ceiling, 'Adjectives agree with nouns.' I bet that lesson went home all right.

So much, as I said, for the structure. What about the furniture?

You can't do much about the age or the quality of it, unless you set out to make the Bursar's life, or the governors' lives, a misery – and that won't do much for your promotion prospects. All you can do, realistically, beyond keeping your cupboards looking tidy, is to decide how you want it placed? And even that is limited if you have to share the use of the room with another member of staff.

However, if the room is really yours, all the time, what are you going to do?

Fashions and ideas on this topic change. They change quite rapidly, and quite often. A teacher with long experience can be faced with room arrangement fashions coming round full circle – and more than once. Whatever I write on this topic now is quite likely to produce frowns, wry shakes of head, explosions of disgust, and eyes raised to the ceiling according to the age, experience, and bonnet bees of the reader.

I shouldn't worry too much about what other people think. If a pattern of furniture suits you, if it springs from your experience and considered views, if you feel it is based on common sense, above all if it helps you to move closer to achieving your teaching aims, and it doesn't harm a pupil, then go ahead. As far as I am aware, headmasters, advisers, inspectors, and other authority figures do not yet stand in the classroom and issue specific instructions about individual chairs, benches, desks, and tables, so you have freedom.

There have been occasions when I have come away from a meeting or a course or a seminar, feeling, shall we say, a little 'down' because it was looking as if I was moving away from the mainstream of modern progressive thought, or that it was quietly moving away from me. But I was always able to console myself with the thought that I could still go back into my own classroom and do what I thought, in my bones, was right, and nobody ever came in to order me to do otherwise.

So with the geography of your classroom – where they are actually sitting? Of course the very size of the room and the sheer number of pupils are immovable. Something else you have to 'lump'. But do you want them sitting singly or in pairs? Do you insist on merging the sexes or separating them? Do you value the contentment of friends sitting together or do you think constant chatting is a pain? Do you take care to break up little enclaves of sedition, or do you content yourself with parking the worst offender at the front, right under your desk?

How much do you value the fact that you can see all their faces, at the same time, all the time? Are you prepared to tolerate, not straight rows and columns of desks, but a patchwork of little junctions of tables, with pupils ranged round them like members of a board meeting? So that, at any one time, you can never look more than half of them in the eye? (With the others, you have to be content with shoulder blades.) Yes, I know, this may sound a little 'loaded'. You may have good reasons for such an arrangement. OK – it's your classroom.

How often do you need to have them all listening to

you, eye to eye? How often do you want to talk to them as a group?

One could go on. Different ages may require different arrangements. Different abilities. Different subjects. Different topics *within* a subject.

As I said with the doors and the walls, think of the whole picture. There may be freedoms and options available which perhaps had not occurred to you before.

Consider your own desk, or table, or high stool, or whatever antique relic or modern tubular freak you have had foisted on you. It ought to be a sort of focus. Nobody expects a class to be gazing at a teacher in rapt attention all the time, but the facility to command that attention must be available *if needed*.

I suggest that height is a factor worth considering. Ask yourself, why do cavalrymen look so damned superior? Because they are higher up. I am not suggesting that you lord it like Genghis Khan. Just that it helps if they can all see you. If you are slightly higher up, they can. If your desk or table is at floor level like theirs, some of them won't find it easy to do so, because there will be bodies in the way.

All right, so a teacher can always stand up. But there are many times when he needs to conduct business sitting down – going through an exercise with a pupil, taking in a set of marks, and so on.

This is where a simple dais can be precious. Only six or eight inches, but it makes a difference. And of course, if you use it when you were standing as well, so much the better. I'm sure there is some kind of psychological factor at work if they are not looking towards you but looking *up* at you.

Once again we are back to the element of the unconscious. Height means something. They don't consciously notice it, but you are having an effect. One hears more of short people resenting their lack of inches than one does of tall people bemoaning their excess of them.

I did not appreciate the value of a dais till I moved into a new room and found one. Not all the rooms in my corridor had one. When I had to take the odd lesson for an absent teacher in another further up the corridor, it dawned on me. I came to value it. Then came a great re-shuffle organised from on high. Once again I had to lump it. I had to move to the other side of the school. There was a colleague who, I heard, coveted my room (it was bigger than all the others in the corridor.) So I thought, 'Well, I have to go, and I can't stop that man moving in to 'my' territory. But he's not going to have my dais.' I drummed up a secret task force of large boys. Sir's dais vanished from Room One, and mysteriously turned up in my new room. It was that important.

One final thought, about classroom bureaucracy, or geography. I have often stressed the value of thinking small. Well, here's one exception: Think for a moment of the whole class, the whole lesson. Think big.

The weather gets hot. If our weather experts are to be believed, we may have to accept the increased frequency of such a phenomenon. Consider, as Joe would say. Your windows are open. Your door is gaping. It's still hot. The boys have still been playing football, and even the girls are 'glowing'. Why not migrate outside to that inviting grass?

'No,' said one of my headmasters, in a memorable response. 'If it's too hot to be indoors, it's too hot to be outdoors.'

16 Getting to know you

'ON THE WHOLE, KNOWLEDGE is preferable to ignorance.' This was one of the deceptively innocent, but in fact, mightily profound, observations that Sir Kenneth Clark offered in the concluding programme of his famous television series 'Civilisation'. I have quoted it before, and I think it worth quoting again.

It is not the greatest quotation in the world, and one could easily debate the validity of it (harassed secretaries of debating societies could well be glad to snap it up as likely fodder for a society's winter programme).

In the context of teaching, though, it seems pretty undebatable; knowledge has a bedrock place in the activities of the profession. In this particular case, I do not refer to what the teacher knows about his subject or his profession, but to what the teacher knows about his pupils. It is surely incumbent upon him to find out as much about them as the timetable and research in free periods permit.

That demands a share of his attention. However, I would also suggest that he spares a little thought for the business of how well he wants *them* to know *him*.

You, the teacher, have probably more control over this than of any other feature of your teaching life. Though, perhaps less than a few decades ago, because of the ubiquity now of social media and the proliferation of digital knowledge. We are constantly being battered by revelatory articles which have the potential to scare us half to death with 'news' of how much people know about us – and we don't even know they know it half the time.

There isn't much you can do about that, as I said, but there is something you can do about how much you give away in your day-to-day dealings with a class.

I'm going to mix a fine recipe of metaphors now: by all means take off the lid and show them the works now and again. But don't lay too many cards on the table. Let them into some (carefully-chosen) trade secrets, but not into personal ones. I've got to the point at last.

To put it as simply as possible, talk about the work, but don't talk about yourself. That sounds easy to keep to, but a whole class bursting with good humour and cheerful cheek can pose a deadly trap. They are past-masters at what may be called 'diversionary interrogation'. Most of us can be tempted sometimes to talk about ourselves, and a class can be very adept at kidding you that they are dying to hear what you have to say. Watch out. You are not in fact the object of intense human interest; you are simply being steered joyfully away from the business of work, from the agenda. It makes a wonderful interlude, verging on entertainment.

We once had a History teacher – clearly a very clever man – who had worked for many years as a boffin in the science of radar (when it was an exciting novelty) before switching to teaching. To our great joy, he turned out to be a sitting duck for this diversionary interrogation. What he had to say, as it happened, was fascinating to a group of young teenage boys, but we didn't learn much History.

Here is another splendid example of what a paradox young people can be. They can display Machiavellian subtlety when it comes to teasing information out of a teacher who may not be fully aware of what is going on, and yet they can also be vulnerable to the most childlike credulity when presented with information about another teacher – from a different source.

Take the credulity. A teacher once told me about a seasoned practitioner he had met in his very first school. It was a tough school, and most of the staff had trouble at one time or another. But this veteran had none at all. Naturally, our beginner asked him what his secret was, and was surprised when the veteran told him so readily.

'Well,' he said, 'there is a very strong impression at large in the school that I once held a thirteen-year-old boy out of a window by his hair. I have never seen fit to deny this story.' It worked like a charm. Whenever the noise level showed a tendency to rise beyond tolerable levels, all this man had to do was walk towards a window, and at once a sepulchral silence descended.

Or again, I had a colleague about the same age as myself, and there was a body of belief going the rounds that he had been a squadron leader in the War, which would have put him at a good twenty years older than he actually was. They are not good at judging ages.

I could go on, but will content myself with the tale of another teacher we had who suffered from a degree of spasticity, which made his limbs jerk markedly when he walked. Shortly after I joined the school, I was informed with dark earnestness of the reason for this disability: he had trodden on a land mine.

There must be as many such stories as there are schools. It is difficult sometimes to accept that such gullibility can co-exist in a class of pupils whose skill at extracting information would make an MI5 interrogator of double-agents seem like Mrs. Tiggywinkle.

So watch out. Be warned. Keep the shutters handy. If you do let anything out, it should be rare, minimal, deliberate, and for a good reason. Above all, it should be your idea. You have offered it; they have not prised it out of you. And after you have let it out, there should still be plenty of mystery left.

Remember that it is your job not only to keep order, but to keep distance. A dash of mystery helps to keep that distance. It adds to their interest. They should be made to realise that there is plenty more left that you haven't shown. Shed all the secrets, and they think they have you all buttoned up. You have opened the door to familiarity. It will be only a matter of time before someone takes a liberty, and you will be scrambling, red-faced, to scoop up shards of shattered dignity off the floor.

That is all very well, but the fact remains that a teacher must be accessible. Ice has to be broken. Warmth has to be generated. They have to feel that they are dealing with a human being. I have also said elsewhere in this book – probably more than once – that one of the things they value in a teacher is simply getting on with it. Being get-at-able, being busy.

I still stand by that. We are back to the balance again. In amongst all the 'getting on with it', there should also be a drop or two of lubrication, if for nothing else but to ease things along. If you like, it's a sort of etiquette. Like saying 'Good morning'. They are human (despite what the cynics say), and while they are getting out books and hiding smartphones they appreciate a spot of 'easing into it' like everybody else.

Well, if you don't talk about yourself or tell elaborate stories, or try too hard to get friendly, what *do* you do?

You do what everybody else does when they meet people: you talk about nothing in particular. It's hardly demanding.

The weather is a good standby, especially if it is extreme, and, from what we are being told, this will become easier and easier in the coming years. There should be a natural disaster somewhere or other, and you can pick a prodigy from that. Again, we are rarely short of political scandals, lurid court cases, pop stars' divorces, or Eurovision song contests. It doesn't have to be elaborate; it needs to last only for twenty seconds. But you're away. You have renewed relations; you have picked up old contacts. It's all unobtrusive; it's so familiar they hardly know it's happening. They're used to it. They are comfortable. You too look as if you are comfortable. Every little helps.

And, with all these little things that you can talk about, almost as neighbours over the garden wall, out of twenty-five or thirty of them, somebody will always have something to say.

Domestic chat is useful too. Once in an English lesson, I was reminded (I can't remember why) about a wayward carpet we once owned that had a habit of 'walking' towards the fireplace. I told them about it. A boy put up his hand and said that they had a carpet in their lounge that did exactly the same thing. This boy was rarely stimulated to offer a contribution to the conversation, but this time he did, and he was quite animated – thanks purely to my mentioning a disobedient carpet. It had moved him to join in. That, surely, was a good thing. Tiny, tiny…

Each of these minibits merges to create an effect, the nucleus of a class atmosphere. At the risk of sounding a little precious, it brings the class slightly closer together. It gives them just an inch more common ground. It adds to the class joint personality. And it's all unconscious. They don't know it's happening. So there is nothing to object to.

And they haven't got around to thinking up ways of taking your mind off the lesson. At that particular moment, there isn't any discernible lesson to take the mind off.

Remember a basic truth. There is one of you, and a roomful of them. No matter how closely you try to keep your cards close to your chest, you are displaying your personality every time you listen, ask, comment, correct, or shout. You can't help it. They are going to form an impression. All you can do is hope that the impression is a favourable one.

There are twenty or thirty pairs of eyes (sharp eyes) on you all the time; by the end of the lesson, they will between them have noticed pretty well all there is to notice. Even if those eyes are not on you, and their bored owners are gazing out of the window, or looking at the clock, or tolerating a droning voice, they will have formed an impression.

That impression is the result of what you have been doing, or not doing. If you would like to improve that impression, then you have to change what you are doing. In other words, try to make yourself a better teacher.

Perhaps one or two things I have been talking about in other chapters may help towards that end. The 'world' you have chosen to live and work in is like all the other worlds that other people live in. There is no justice; it takes all sorts; you just put up with it. Boring, eternal, and true. Every success brings in its wake a fresh set of problems. There is no end.

However, if you have done your best, listened to, and evaluated, all the advice, there may be yet one more tactic you can try in the eternal campaign. That's what you are doing – campaigning. That's what they should see you as

– a campaigner. Not a friend, a confidant, a hand-holder – a campaigner. More, a campaigner they don't fully understand. Always keep one last little trick up your sleeve – the ability to surprise them. Everybody needs a shock now and then. Keep your shock equipment polished and ready. Wheedle and cajole, comfort and cosset; explain and explain however many times it takes – all these things, and more. Chase and chivvy; rap the knuckles, bark when necessary. But – just once in a while – you'll know when – bite.

It doesn't have to be harsh or frightening. Just unexpected. And justified. However comfy the atmosphere, remember it's still them and you. It's your class, not theirs. You run the show.

And, really, they like it that way.

17 The question of bad pupils

ONE OF THE MANY things on which I am not an expert is the training of young soldiers today to become officers. However, I can, as it happens, tell you a thing or two about the training of young soldiers to become officers several decades ago. It doesn't matter much just how long ago; anyone who has experienced training carried out by the Army soon discovers that it has built into it an element of unforgettability. Right or wrong, good or bad, you don't forget.

That's the first point.

The second is that the passage of the years does not necessarily devalue the experience of those years. The past need not be, by pure definition, irrelevant. Times do indeed change. So do attitudes, methods, science, technology, philosophy, and no doubt many other things too. That does not automatically render one's memories of them valueless; certain constants remain. Young trainee officers today have to face, and overcome, the same problems as their fathers and grandfathers did all those years ago in at least one major respect. Whatever decade or century they are in, young officers must learn to lead men (and now women too) in action. That inescapable fact must colour their training.

So if I call up a memory of my own military training, I suggest that it still has some validity.

As officer cadets, we had it drummed into us time and time again that 'there is no such thing as bad soldiers; only bad officers'. I put to the court therefore this question: 'Can the same be said about pupils and teachers?'

How far is it true that 'there is no such thing as bad pupils; only bad teachers'?

A first response would be – at my guess the most likely response – that it all depends on what you mean by 'bad'. Far from easing the answer, such an assertion would seem to make the problem initially much worse; the Shorter Oxford English Dictionary devotes an entire column to the word.

No chapter – indeed no book – on teaching is likely to be of much use if it attempts to do justice to the myriad implications of the word 'bad' in this context. Common sense has to be applied.

So out will have to go synonyms like 'overripe', 'counterfeit', 'stale', 'cruel', 'immoral', 'inclement', 'depraved', and a dozen more.

Then there are the near-miss epithets for pupils: 'slow', 'incompetent', 'late', 'fussy', 'disorganised', 'forgetful', 'lazy'. And plenty of others; look at the heartfelt comments of tired teachers on old-time reports.

And yet many of these verdicts do not necessarily mean that it is all the pupil's fault. If he really is slow, for instance, well, the chances are that you and he are stuck with it. If an educational philosopher could come up with a recipe for making kids brighter, it would constitute something of a disturbance in the whole world of education (to say nothing of medicine and psychology). If he is late, perhaps a bumbling parent or a half-baked bus company are to blame. And so on.

No. Let us be practical. What we are talking about, really, is behaviour. How much are they to blame for that? How culpable are they for activities and attitudes which make the conduct of a classroom lesson increasingly difficult? Or to what extent has the teacher brought such a difficult situation upon himself?

When things get troublesome, and you're feeling tired and besieged, it is easy, in your morbid evening gloom, in front of a guttering gas fire, to hunch yourself over your bedtime beverage, and feel sorry for yourself. You find yourself fastening on to a fact or an event or a person – or a series of them – and you see in them the cause of all the trouble… if only they were different… Before long the room becomes littered with all the crosses you have to bear.

Time to get a grip, isn't it? Time to remind yourself of some realities. Like the best generals, get to know, and to understand, 'the enemy'. Remember what I said in another chapter: that what pervades the classroom is a semi-permanent state of friendly, undeclared war. If you have drawn the short straw, perhaps not even very friendly.

What are they? They are young. They are loud. They are impulsive. They are impressionable. They are volatile. They take up a lot of room. Above all, they are immature. It is pointless to expect much adult behaviour from them. It is true that they are capable of great heights, and also of great depths, but that is simply proof of their volatility.

However you regard these qualities and propensities, you have to accept that you are not going to change them. That is them. You have to accommodate yourself to it, and you go on from there. Sitting up late with the bedtime cocoa and working out brilliant scenarios which will magically solve the crisis tomorrow won't help. You'll forget. And even if you remember, it won't work; it never does.

Don't burn the midnight oil pining for what you would like it to be. Steel yourself to what it is. Don't make yourself miserable about something you can't achieve. Remind yourself what you are there for. To deliver education. The goods. You are not there to like them. Or to make them nice. Any more than they are there to like you. (And I doubt very much if any of them have given much thought to making you nice.)

Your job is to work together. Everything else takes second place. Who is 'good' and who is 'bad' is largely irrelevant. All you are seeking is a classroom atmosphere settled enough for you to get across the facts and attitudes you need to. Everything else is a bonus.

You will get trouble; of course you will. No class is perfect. Sometimes, equally truly and equally inevitably, you will have asked for it. But it is the failures you learn from, not the successes. That's why you should never be afraid, or ashamed, of failures. They will have done you a good turn. You may not get it right next time, but at least you won't get it wrong again in the same way. You are no doubt familiar with the old chestnut that the man who never made a mistake never made anything.

Now and again, remember your own worth. You know what you are trying to achieve in the classroom, and you know how and why you chose to be there. That gives you a dignity, which they cannot but notice.

You are a trier. You must be, or you would have given up long ago. You want to get better. No teacher *wants* to get worse. True, there are some teachers who are content to slumber in the rut they have eroded for themselves, and they are no great advert for the profession. But they are usually observable, and avoidable. Entertaining curiosities. But no probationer would have thought of emulating them. I once had a colleague who took some of his PE lessons *sitting down.* It would have been interesting to find out what the pupils thought of him. I doubt if many of his colleagues took him seriously.

Accept what you are – imperfect. Will you make them perfect pupils? No, of course not. Just go in and do what you know you have to do. Don't necessarily parade your shortcomings, but don't cower behind them either. If you are there doing your job, they will see that you are doing your job, and will accept you for what you are. If they don't respond to that, at least your conscience is clear.

They will have much more time for a cheerful trier, even a hamfisted trier, than they will for a sad sack with 'Victim' and 'Martyr' written all over him. Yet another reason why you hold most of your cards close to your chest. They are not interested in your midnight moods of despair or your migraines or your sick headaches. If you make a meal of them, you are inviting advantage to be taken of you.

Consider the story of the masochist and the sadist:

The gloomy masochist said to the observant sadist, 'Go on. Hit me.'

The sadist looked at him for a while, and then said, very thoughtfully, 'No.'

Let us return to the original proposition. As with so many such propositions, despite its glibness, it deserves consideration. Even deserves to be taken seriously. But not too seriously. The willing teacher can submit himself to a regime of self-improvement just so far.

While he is doing that, experience will teach him to deal with criticism. He learns to fend off the routine shafts, the cliché quips.

For example, if someone exaggerates the importance

of an instance where a pupil caught him out in a simple matter of fact, the answer is: 'It is not my job to know; it is my job to make sure that *they* know.' [It appears that he had succeeded.]

We are still a long way from a satisfactory answer to the riddle.

Common sense, logic, psychology, and historians could all probably make the case that really nasty people do exist. If they do, it would follow that really nasty pupils exist as well. Though not as many as we would estimate in the depths of our persecution complex evenings with the cocoa.

If, however, you should be unlucky enough to meet such a creature, I'm afraid I have no treatment to offer, much less a cure – except possibly a quiet disembowelling behind the bike sheds. But that is not to be recommended, and in any case you would only be able to resort to it once. No chance there to build a slick technique.

The guide book is not yet written which tells you how to anticipate every crisis, avoid every sling and arrow of outrageous fortune (or outrageous pupil), and guard against every dose of bad luck.

The best I can do is offer just a few hints. First, remember you are not alone. You do not have to take him on by yourself. Second, if he is asking for trouble, don't give it to him. If he revels in confrontation, that needs two people: he is one and you are the other. Don't respond. You are not there to make up the party. Do not get drawn into a feud.

Even if you register a success, the chances are that he will not be cowed by just one setback. He will return for a second round; his pride will not allow him to do otherwise.

His priorities are all about winning, not about learning. It is most unlikely that you will succeed by means of a face-to-face encounter.

This principle applies, incidentally, to disagreements at a much milder level too. Never go down into the arena unless you are utterly, completely, absolutely sure of winning. And how often does that happen?

What do you do then? You use the system. Don't look forward to a tiny triumph in a local shootout; bring the big guns to bear. That's what they are there for. With the really unpleasant cases, you are fighting to defend the system, not just yourself.

And, as I have said above, no success is guaranteed. Many serious cases do not end with all the stray threads neatly tied up. Be prepared for incompleteness, dissatisfaction, and quite possibly some residual frustration.

A final thought. You may find this whole business distasteful, and the machinery of maintaining discipline and general order a constant burden. If it looks like dominating your working life, that is no way to go about teaching, no matter how knowledgeable and willing you may have been to start with.

Being prepared to consider a change of direction is no shame. Not everybody is cut out to be a salesman or a missionary. Nor with teaching. Not shameful. Sensible.

18 Little bits of business

Work, as we all know, gives you experience. A very worthwhile and truly remarkable commodity – experience. Obtaining it is not a simple procedure. It is not available just anywhere. You can't go out and buy it in a shop. You can't steal it. (You can steal knowledge, but you can't steal experience; it is up to you to turn knowledge *into* experience.) You can't hire it or borrow it. You can use somebody else's up to a point, if they are generous enough, but ultimately it is not the solution. It is not really yours; it is second-hand. You need the effort of getting it for it to work properly. You can't even download it from the internet or buy it on Amazon.

It can be frustrating that some of the most valuable things are so elusive. You can't make it happen; you must wait for it to turn up. It's like contentment or happiness or love; you just have to do your best and hope for the best.

Watch out for its arrival, from whatever unexpected direction. Never look askance at it, even when it arrives from an unlikely source and is heavily disguised as adversity. Cherish it all. Gather it, hoard it, keep it safe, and keep in mind those rainy days in the future when you are going to need it. Never reject it. No experience is ever wasted.

So much for the 'moral of the day'.

But it is so useful, isn't it? I have put it in here, at the top of the page, because it the mainspring of three things, all of which are vital to your progress and survival as a teacher: knowledge, ideas, and confidence. (Luckily too, the equation works both ways; each can generate the other.)

I'll say it again – knowledge, ideas, and confidence.

Don't neglect opportunities to widen your knowledge (oh dear, this is so obvious, isn't it?) Of course knowledge matters. People respect knowledge. Pupils, somewhat surprisingly, also respect knowledge.

My school, like many others after the War, had rather more downs than ups. We had a bad spell among our French teachers, when several of them came and went with surprising rapidity. We didn't have the chance to become acquainted with any of them – well, very little – but, like most pupils, we were prepared to give each one the benefit of the doubt for a while, till he showed form. But there was one of them who gave the clear impression very early on that he didn't know much. My abiding memory of him was the fact he needed to look up the right word in the back of the book an inordinate number of times. Our regard for him dropped like a stone.

This was probably an unfair judgment; schoolboys can be very unfair, we know. The chances are that we were too quick to judge. But the point still holds: rightly or wrongly, fairly or unfairly, we decided that he didn't know enough to be teaching us French. We may have been little philistine ignoramuses, but we did know enough to be aware that knowledge was important. And he didn't seem to have much.

It follows then that the more you can collect, the more advantage you have, and in the classroom you can do with all the advantage you can get. Remember that semi-permanent state of friendly undeclared war.

Even when you think you know the subject like the back of your hand, there should always be room for a spot more knowledge (here I go – moralising again – sorry).

But honestly, it's true; you can pick up scraps of useful material from the most unlikely places.

The more facts you have at your fingertips, the more likely one of them will trigger an idea. Better still, you can come across a *pair* of facts, and suddenly you will see a connection, an implication, a new way ahead. Sparks fly between the two, and suddenly you have a third. The more facts you have at your disposal, the more likely that is to happen. Presto – you have an idea.

If that new idea works, it cannot but be good for your confidence.

How's this for an example? Suppose you are teaching the French Revolution. Which I have done many times. What do you have to get across? The 'big' things like inequitable taxation, the blue blood tradition, the unsuitability of both King and Queen for their position, the outbreak, the Bastille episode, the new assemblies, the Rights of Man, the war, the Reign of Terror, and so on. All the bread-and-butter history of the Revolution. A big dollop of economics and politics.

Well, one day I picked up a book about capital punishment. A long way away from the National Assembly and the attempted flight of the Royal Family. But it had some extremely colourful stuff in it about the guillotine. This was perfect fodder for a blood-and-thunder digression – about early attempts to decapitate by the sword, the different embryonic designs for the guillotine's blade, experiments to determine whether there was any life remaining in the severed head. And more.

This was tailor-made for the sensation technique. I could announce that I was going to talk to them for ten solid minutes without any of them uttering a syllable or stirring a limb; I could guarantee total silence. It worked like a charm every time. All those pins dropped with a noise like a tin tray.

All right, it was a great big joke (if a rather macabre one), and there was never any suggestion that it would replace the bread and butter. But it caught them, it held them, it taught them something, and, bloodthirsty little beasts that they were, entertained them. And I bet they remembered it. If they remember something like that, there are greater chances that they will remember the rest of the lesson, if only by unconscious association of ideas, and the more likely they will be to remember you.

One of the ponderous pieces of advice I regularly passed on to the training college students we used to have with us for a term at a time was: 'Try and find a way to make yourself memorable.' Particularly as a History teacher.

Knowledge, ideas, confidence. They all grow with usage. The more knowledge you gather, the more likely it is that that new knowledge will generate ideas. The more ideas you have the more you can give variety and freshness to your teaching. The more success these ideas have, the more your confidence grows, as you build a little arsenal of tactics which you know, barring accidents, will help them to enjoy your lesson, remember you, and be willing to come back for more.

Don't neglect an opportunity. Don't let them go to waste. With time and practice, you will be able to build a tiny bag of tricks, which you can carry with you like a tool kit.

Work on them; refine them; polish them; trim them; make them more streamlined each time you use them.

If they really are proper, honest-to-goodness tricks, make sure you can rely on them to work every time. There is nothing worse for your rhythm and morale than the trick that *doesn't* work.

If your tactic does work, what have you achieved? Success. And we all know that nothing succeeds like success. They now know that 'Sir' can do something besides mark exercise books and memorise theorems – whether performing a prodigious piece of mental arithmetic, exhibiting a display of memory, telling a cracking good story (it doesn't have to be funny), sharing a strong experience, pulling a rabbit out of a hat – anything.

Curiously, it doesn't matter much if you've done it before; if it's good and watchable, they are happy to enjoy it again. If we go to a variety performance, we don't turn up our noses at seeing the lady sawn in half once more. We can relish it just as much a second and third time. It can benefit from its very familiarity.

Related to that is another item you can slip in when you think the time is right, or the opportunity presents itself: they like being shown trade secrets – or what they think are trade secrets. (It helps if the teacher has a dash of the con artist about him. He should have; he's been around a lot longer than they have.) Like everybody else, they love having the lid taken off and being shown the works. You don't need to have examples spelt out by someone like me; every subject has its own selection of potential trump cards.

It doesn't have to be the Great Giveaway. You have been in the trade long enough to know which cats can be safely let out of the bag. With the vital stuff, no, discretion is the order of the day – every day. Not only do you not let out the big cats; you don't tell them which cats are in the bag. You don't even tell them there's a bag.

It's another way of preparing them for the adult status that is coming their way. They need to learn that adults have a world of their own, just as the young have a world of *their* own. Both worlds are equally valid and worthy of respect. And private.

It is difficult to specify further. If you keep your radar working, almost anything you come across, anywhere, can be appropriated. Every little embellishment to the lesson makes you that little bit more interesting. They are pleased to have a teacher with one or two surprises up his sleeve. Anything is welcome which breaks the monotony.

But – there's always a 'but' – remember that this whole idea, technique, tactic (call it what you will) is only a weapon, not **the** weapon. You must be in total control of it at all times. Don't get carried away by your own cleverness. They will rumble you.

The bag of tricks is just that, and no more. Keep it all in balance. Once again we come back to balance. There is still no substitute for good, old-fashioned explanation, questioning, repetition, practice – in other words, work.

What I have discussed in this chapter is the equivalent of the twiddly bits that make a musical performance just a little more catchy. That is all it is. Don't get too fond of it. It's easy to get quite good at it, and then temptation yawns in your path. Ration it. Keep it rare. If you never did a single twiddly bit, and you kept up a high level of consistent work, they would still respect you. Work can thrive without the twiddly bits. Twiddly bits without the work can't.

However, just to swing back yet again, my main point

is still sound: you can't beat experience, knowledge, and ideas. They can lead to consistent achievement as well as temptation. And the dividend of confidence is priceless.

One last idea. Don't be afraid to employ your own specialist knowledge and your own personality. If there is something you're good at, try and take advantage of it. Only you can know what those things are. It can be anything – manual dexterity, musical skill, sheer memory, rare specialised knowledge, draughtsmanship, knowledge won from previous employment. But keep it rationed, under control.

Think further. A habit, a catch-phrase, a saying, a little ritual, a favourite oath – any tiny, but apparently casual, affectation. It must spring from what you are. You can't invent it. If you do, it will show, they will spot it at once, and you will be imitated for the wrong reason. It must simply 'grow', like Topsy. Something you can throw off without effort, almost without thinking.

All part of the quest to make the lesson just a little more worth listening to. If you like, the icing-sugar of learning. But choose your main ingredients well; it's what's *inside* the cake that counts.

19 What to do with advice

THE TOPIC OF ADVICE is a great loosener of the tongue. Everybody, it seems, has something to say under the heading of 'Advice'. While I was searching for a way to get this chapter started, my daughter-in-law was pottering about the kitchen making tea.

I asked her a question relating to the advice she had been given about her work. Now, my daughter-in-law is not a loquacious lady, but she stopped making the tea, reflected for an appreciable interval, and then launched herself into three or four continuous minutes of observations on the matter, without any marked pauses or promptings from me.

People find advice easy to talk about. They also find it easy to give. From what one hears of it, one is tempted to wonder whether the willingness to offer advice on a subject might vary in inverse proportion to the knowledge of it. Put another way, the real expert is reluctant to hold forth, because he has such a wide command of the subject, and he knows where the gaps in his knowledge are. He knows how much he doesn't know, and so is unwilling to say too much in case he gives an unbalanced, and therefore unhelpful, view.

This may explain the genesis of well-known – nay, notorious – pieces of advice offered by world experts who know that they haven't got time to put it all into words, so they distil a smart little observation about it which has to satisfy the interviewer at the time.

The anthologies are full of remarks like these:

Q. How do you become a good batsman?

A. You just put the bat to the ball.

Q. How do you become a good actor?
A. Learn the lines and don't bump into the furniture.
Q. How do you become a good writer?
A. You tell the tale.
Q. How do you get good poetry published?
A. Write it.
Q. How do you become a good orchestral conductor?
A. Don't take your left hand out of your waistcoat pocket, and never smile encouragingly at the brass.
Q. How do you stage the opera *Il Trovatore*?
A. Easy. All you need is the four greatest opera singers in the world.

Yes, these comments are direct, honest, and heartfelt, and based on deep experience. But they are also smart, slick, and quotable, as the perpetrators were no doubt well aware, and quite possibly intended them to be. They are therefore suspect. Chew them over, but don't swallow them whole. They contain some truth, but nothing like the whole truth.

The same principle applies to teaching. There is as much advice about teaching out there as there is about almost any other human activity. Be aware of it, study it, use it, but all the while preserve your wits at concert pitch. Keep your head screwed on; don't let it get turned.

There is another part of the truth that you must never neglect – your own judgment. Remember the emperor's new clothes.

Say you obtain a book about teaching. Look at the blurb on the back. Is there a picture of the author there? What does he look like? What impression do you get? Like a political party candidate's hand-out in a local election, it's not much, but it's what you've got to go on. What does it say about his career or his credentials? What does it suggest about his intentions in the introduction?

Now read his book. What does he actually say? How well does he say it? If nothing else it ought to be clear and well written. He's a teacher, remember; he has been spending years training pupils to express themselves clearly. If it's not clear and well written, it doesn't say much for his philosophy. If his writing is woolly, his thinking is probably woolly too. If so, why should this man be a professor of education, able to influence movers and shakers at a very high level, and produce widespread changes in schools which are going to influence the lives of your children?

If he hasn't spent much time teaching in a humdrum classroom, who the hell does he think he is, to be telling you how to be a better teacher? It can be quite frightening to discover how little classroom experience some so-called experts (and influential experts) have in fact to their credit. At a humble level, I had a colleague who had, like thousands of others, attended a two-year course at a teacher training college. She told me that not one of her lecturers – not one – had any experience whatever of teaching at an ordinary school. Imagine – transfer this situation to a training hospital, and think of the implications.

Here is an appropriate place to offer a word on language. More specifically, jargon. Every profession is infected with it, and teaching is well up in the jargon-incidence league. I have never met anyone who says he likes it, which of course adds to the mystery of why we tolerate it. Alas, it seems to be a natural, near-unstoppable growth, like moss, or verdigris, or mould.

Fortunately, it is easily recognisable, so we hardly need

the advice to beware of it. We give ourselves a sort of safety-valve of humour, to ease the itch of it by quoting our own, personally-discovered, favourite examples. Here is one of mine.

A group of us (teachers) were discussing the subject in a conference break, and one of our number weighed in with this. He was a History teacher, if memory serves. But it doesn't matter; it could have been one of many subjects. This teacher wanted a few simple drawings to illustrate some notes he had prepared for distribution in some homework project. He was not the best of draughtsmen himself, and by good fortune found out that a boy in the class had some marked talent in this direction. The boy agreed to do the drawings for him.

He was telling a colleague of this stroke of luck, and showed him how good the pictures were. 'It was very good of the lad. Look. They're much better than anything I could have done.'

The colleague in question was one of the modernists who read all the way-out articles in way-out magazines, and was up with all the latest catchwords. Let us call him Mr. Followfad.

Mr. Followfad leaned down and frowned fiercely by way of examination of the drawings while the teacher explained his good luck. When Mr. Followfad spoke, he made no reference to the luck, the willingness of the boy, or the obvious merit of the drawings. Instead he nodded learnedly as if it were no surprise to him, and said, 'Ah, yes – child-orientated resources.'

The teacher telling the story spread his hands and said, 'Child-orientated resources. God Almighty! The kid did the drawings!'

While we are about it, let us also slip in a word about fashion. The world of education seems to me to be particularly vulnerable to the dictates of it. It is my impression that professions like medicine, pharmacology, engineering, and no doubt many others, pursue a forward career which goes from one innovation to another, often with bewildering speed, whereas education appears to go not forward but in cycles. Indeed, it is a truism in teaching that, if you stand still long enough, the world comes round to you all over again.

An example? I forget how many years ago, a group of schools in my area was smitten by a new gospel in History teaching. The idea was that classes were to be taught not singly but in pairs. In one of their two weekly periods the two classes were taught separately, and in the second period they were amalgamated. During the obligatory 'course' we had to attend, the finer points of this revolutionary system were expounded to us, and virtues like flexibility, scope for individual teaching, 'incentivisation', and many others, were extolled in full measure. It was of course an innovation that was ground-breaking, and would take forward the teaching of History in the county by leaps and bounds.

I was new to the area, so I minded my manners and paid due attention. But I noticed at the back of the room in the 'Teachers' Centre' a gentleman of mature years, who was giving the proceedings only minimal recognition. By no stretch of imagination could the expression on his face be described as 'animated'.

We happened to exchange a few words afterwards as we put on our coats, and I ventured to refer to the fact that he had not exactly wriggled with excitement during the talk.

He wound his scarf round his neck. 'We did all this thirty years ago. Didn't last long.'

The same thing applies to the debate on mixed ability. Fashion.

When I first came to teach in North Devon, the comprehensive gospel was catching fire. Everything was to be fair. All playing fields were to be 'level'. No child was to be 'labelled'. 'Stream' became a dirty word. No child was to be put up or put down. They were all 're-allocated'. All moves were sideways. Every child was to become more equal than everybody else.

There was no question here of teachers being given 'advice'; they were told. Mixed ability was the way forward.

I have no professional experience of educational administration, and I have no access to county statistics, so I have to rely on personal observation, conversation with colleagues, press reports whose reliability is as questionable as it has always been, general gossip, and seat-of-the-pants impressions. Given those provisos, my general feeling is that trying to find a vigorous lobby for mixed ability now would be rather like looking for a Nazi after the War.

Whether I am right or wrong does not matter; advice on a topic like this, for a young teacher, would not seem to be particularly valuable.

Although I have been at pains to show how much advice is available, I hope I have also made it clear that much of that advice is of doubtful merit. Which once again throws you, the teacher, back on his own resources. (Here I am repeating myself once again.)

And why not? One of the merits of the English system,

for all its alleged shortcomings, is that a teacher, so long as he observes the law of the land, can still do pretty much what he wants to do in the privacy of his own classroom.

This is the power-house, the nerve centre, the place that matters – the classroom. I have mentioned the gaps in my knowledge several times, but I do know a bit about what happens between a teacher, on his own, in a room, and a group of young people, day in day out, week in week out, helping them to learn. That is where the graft is, where the grief is, and where the satisfaction is. If you come across any advice which enhances any of that, it might be worth listening to.

Be aware, then, and be wary, of these two bogeymen – jargon and fashion. You will never avoid them completely. And, to be over-fair, I suppose we must give the fashion fans and the jargoneers the benefit of the doubt; at least they are trying. Trying, that is, to go forward; they can enjoy the righteous advantage of accusing their opponents of being backward.

Now go back to that teacher I spoke about two or three pages ago. Suppose you have, instead of reading his book, attended one of his lectures. You may not have half as many letters after your name as he has, but you can judge perfectly well what sort of speaker he is – forthright or hesitant, upright or hunched, clear or foggy. Can you even hear him? How much slang is there? How many 'like's', how many 'kind-of's', how many 'kindoflikes'? How much does he simply declaim from a script? How many times does he project a series of sentences on to a screen, and then simply recite them? Does he know the difference between speaking and merely talking?

If he has bothered to wear a tie, is it pulled up to his

throat? Are his trousers baggy? Has he donned jeans and white trainers to address an audience of hundreds? Does this help you to form an impression? Do these things matter in your book?

You don't have to be a veteran or a head of department to come to a judgment. Once, at a conference, I was sitting beside a lady of, shall we say, mature years, clearly a lady of poise and character. Her summary of the morning's speaker was: 'That man is wearing his best suit.' Make of that what you will. I know she made something of it.

In the afternoon, we had another speaker, Headmaster of a large comprehensive school in the days when they were quite a socialist government flagship. The same lady observed quietly, 'Now that man is wearing a suit as if he's used to it.' And he was. He looked the part of what the presenters intended him to be.

All these features count. They tell you things.

I will venture further. I suggest that it is possible to get a handle sometimes on a speaker's motives. Is he a sincere reformer, a scholar (this is about education after all), a fluent advocate, basing his remarks on sound research and wide experience? Or does his lecture come off the conveyor belt, punctuated by constant recitings off the screen, frequent quoting from learned journals, and ending with a plug for his latest book? In other words, is he simply career-building?

A final little prediction. If you stay in the profession long enough, and build your portfolio of experience, you could well find yourself at a lecture, or – worse – on a course, where you are better qualified than the speaker.

So, at whatever stage of your career you find yourself, you will be a position to judge. If you are young and inexperienced, so are a lot of other teachers, and what you might say will resonate with quite a lot of people. You are the ones who will influence the profession more than the veterans because you have more time in front of you than those veterans. What you think counts.

Do you accept the advice the prophet offers? If you do, then it won't matter that his shoes are scruffy and he's wearing a rugby shirt and his language is, shall we say 'informal'. You have wisely homed in on the valuable part of his message.

If you don't accept it, then, after what you have just seen, you won't feel surprised, will you?

I have come full circle, to where I say that the value of any advice depends on your individual judgment, for good or ill, for better or worse. It has to make sense to you. You are going to be the one who has to put it over. You will be the one who gets the cheers or the jeers. As I said at the start, if you don't buy it, you won't be able to sell it.

Here I am repeating myself – and probably repeating myself again. Repetition is not necessarily a bad thing. If you like eating a meringue, you take the opportunity to eat another one. If you like a recording of a Mozart symphony, you play it again. If you were bowled over by a film, you go out and buy the DVD. Nothing wrong with that.

Repetition is after all one of the bedrock techniques of teaching. Most of us don't grab it off the bat first time around. A sound piece of advice, then, bears repetition. We learnt our tables by constant recitation. Think how much we memorise from advertising jingles – and we are not even consciously listening. The supreme Nazi propagandist, Joseph Goebbels, affirmed that you maintained control of a population by broadcasting the same message over and over again – people came to believe it, *even if it was a lie.*

If your advice is worthwhile, it does no harm to offer it again. (How often did your parents urge you to clean your teeth?) By the same token, it does no harm to be reminded many times over.

It does no harm either to keep the lines open to all those totally unscientific sources which the experts may not dignify with the word 'advice'. Like instinct. Like that unattractively but evocatively named phenomenon, 'gut reaction'. If it doesn't 'feel' right, the chances are that it isn't. Maybe for others, but not for you. Even more simply – if in doubt, don't.

If a clever remark trembles on your lips, or a daring tactic occurs, and you're not quite sure, that's your instinct telling you something. You haven't missed a chance to be smart; you have used one. There is nothing wrong with underplay and understatement. That means you have plenty in reserve – always a useful trump card up your sleeve. It's hidden but it will show, if you see what I mean.

Of course, you want them to be inspired, forever bursting with eagerness, but these are superlatives, ideals. Don't feel inadequate if you just bowl along most of the time in a friendly, purposeful, well-occupied sort of way. The wisecrackers have a point: learn the lines; tell the tale; put the bat to the ball. The same applies to you: turn up; do the work; cover the ground. Let them look back and see what they have done. If they feel they have got somewhere, then so have you.

When you feel besieged and unnoticed, look out again over the ramparts at the rest of the world. Nine out of ten of us would not go near teaching. You are a minority, a very worthwhile minority. The world needs you. The very, very greatest people in the world's history were teachers.

20 A diversion

It used to be, and for all I know still is, a common practice for Army barracks to turn Christmas Day on its head, and to arrange for Christmas dinner to be served to other ranks by the officers. It is certainly a common enough idea, in many, many societies and cultures, for one day of the year to be set aside for a break, a change, a reversal, for a worship of chaos, a celebration of topsy-turveydom. Well…

Now and again – only occasionally – let one of them do some teaching.

The value of this may be questionable at primary level, though I am happy to be proved wrong here. But in the older classes, especially the sixth form, the concept has mileage. You can't force them; many would quail at the thought. You can hardly blame them; plenty of adults shy away from standing in front of any group of people. In any case, the timetable is rarely elastic enough to allow all of them to have a go. But there may be a few who could be stimulated by the prospect, perhaps even one or two who have had the thought of a teaching career cross their mind.

It also taps into the idea that, now and again, we all like to see the lid taken off and to watch the machinery. In this case, to sit back and look at teaching as a whole. To find out how other people see things.

As always, it is unlikely to work without preparation. Even advance notice. Generate an 'occasion'. Get them interested. Give them freedom of choice on subject matter if you like, but, naturally, it would help if the topics are relevant to the work in hand. Make clear that the job has parameters – standard of work, time allowed, the aim of the lesson, and so on. And knowledge: they have to know something, preferably more than their 'pupils'. There is some mugging up to do. (This is the germ of the idea that if you want to learn a subject, teach it.)

Consider other matters like question technique, testing, general knowledge around the subject or the topic – all if time permits. And, also if time permits, a post-mortem, to which both 'teacher' and 'pupils' contribute.

I omitted from those examples the business of marking, because that is done, generally, outside the lesson. Nevertheless, if it can be fitted in, it can be profitable.

Now this is more advanced stuff, and younger pupils may not have built the experience and maturity to be able to benefit from it. But sixth form, yes. Obviously it will be more applicable in Humanities subjects, where we are considering the composition of extended prose. Though once again I could be wrong. But I have no experience of marking mathematical or scientific or artistic work, so I can't say.

Whatever the subject, prepare. Tell them the idea; tell them how you are going to set it up; tell them how they are to 'play' it; tell them the format of the session; tell them what prospect of progress you are hoping for. Make it clear that you want a bit more than a red pencil mark for bad spelling and absent commas. Proper marking is not mere correction.

Then turn them loose. The essay has been written and handed in. So heads down and they read. There may be a little room for manoeuvre in the way you pair them off – personalities, individual abilities, character, attitude – you alone as the teacher will have the little dash of instinct which tells you that John may benefit from reading Shirley's work, or that Stephanie, always unsure, may have her confidence undermined when she sees Brian's effort, which is several classes above hers.

You keep the tension low by making a joke out of being able to play God and splash the red ink about, but they usually enter into the spirit of it.

The teacher must not be too tickled by the whole thing. It's not the greatest idea in the world, and it is not the infallible key to sensational progress. Once again, timing and advance thought are important. Control, discipline, keep it all on a tight leash.

Don't do something like this early on in the course, I would suggest. You have to be sure of yourself, and of your standing. This is not a joke, a jape, a jolly good wheeze. Don't try it until you've got them tame. If it's early days, and your grip is tenuous, be wary. Worse, if it's late days and your grip is still tenuous, I suggest you don't do it. It will look like a desperate expedient. Here be dragons.

Anyway, let's say it worked. They played ball. They enjoyed the change. What's the profit?

The chances are, you will have risen, if only slightly, in their regard for your creativity. Will they have become skilled markers? Of course not. They won't be able to decide whether the essay is worth ten out of twenty or twelve. But they may surprise themselves by discovering that they can tell the difference between a good essay and a mediocre one – and with luck, *why* it is good or mediocre. They will find that they can home in on waffle or padding or irrelevance, things that the teacher may have taken *them* to task for. As always, it is easier to identify the fault in someone else's work than in your own.

What you are doing, in however slight a way, is building their judgment. You will be asking them to give us the benefit of that judgment, and that is flattering. They know – of course they know – that this is all slight, experimental, tentative, lightweight, and scarcely strategic, but we all have start somewhere on the road to maturity. They all want maturity and command. It is just a tiny step in the right direction. Every little helps..

21 Thinking about teaching

THE SAME QUESTION COULD be asked about almost any occupation, any means of earning a living. What does it do for you? How do you see it? Why do you do it?

Answers will vary according to the mood, position, age, disposition, and circumstances of the 'askee'. For example, I once heard a man who gained his first job during the Depression of the 1930's put it this way: 'In those days, if you had any job at all, you hung on to it.' Not much choice there.

There is the flippant one: I read of a medical man (later admittedly a best-selling humourist), who claimed that he had become an anaesthetist because he was the only member of the team in the operating theatre who was able to do his work sitting down.

There is the shoulder-shrug one ('got to do something'), the holy one ('I was doing what God told me'), the inherited one ('all my family have been --- whatever --- for five generations'), the fatalistic one ('I had been turned down everywhere else'), the rare, single-minded one ('I had wanted to do it since I was seven'), the slightly baffled one ('I sometimes wonder'), and no doubt many, many more.

These answers might vary, too, according to when the question was asked: before embarking on the life's work, during the difficult time of learning the life's work, having, after serious effort, gained respect for the life's work, having gained seniority in the life's work, and finally, looking back on the whole of the life's work, from the vantage point of not having to do it any more.

Teaching can be given this treatment in the same

way as most other means of occupying the major part of the working day. Why teach? There must almost as many answers as there are practitioners. I would not dream of claiming that what follows is anything like a definitive summary of responses. It is simply a sample set of observations that come to mind when I contemplate what amounts to a lifetime in the classroom. Who knows? If I sat down again in a month's time and did the same amount of thinking, I might come up with a different list. The list would never become complete. One cannot continue tacking on afterthoughts for ever.

This little clutch of reactions will do perfectly well to be going on with. Some items here may strike a chord of sympathy or consensus. Others may raise an eyebrow or two. Others again may provoke a shake of the head or a wry smile. One or two, I suppose, may raise the bile (for which I apologise in advance; you can't please everybody).

With that pious proviso, I now offer a few thoughts which occur to me after the work, after the pondering, after the sheer physical fact of having written down nearly 60,000 words about it all. Simply putting words on paper can be a useful stimulant to thought. One thing triggers another. So stand by.

An early point that I was moved to consider came to me when I was listening to the customary speech of thanks delivered some years ago by a very thoughtful lady on the occasion of the farewell present given to her on the day of her retirement. (These items, by the way, are not offered in any implied order of importance; just as I thought of them.)

One of the things she said she valued about teaching was the fact that one had colleagues. That set me thinking.

Obviously I knew perfectly well what colleagues were, and I enjoyed having them, but this lady (I said she was very thoughtful) put the point with particular clarity, and the remembrance stuck. I don't remember much of what she said, but the cogency of her argument impressed me, and has remained since.

Colleagues are special, and not every job of work has them. One's appreciation of their value grows with the years.

Let us begin with making clear what they are not.

They are not friends; they are not neighbours; they are not team mates; they are (obviously) not mere acquaintances; they are not mid-morning coffee-gossipers you see every working day; they are not travelling companions, drinking buddies, bridge-players on commuter trains, or anything else. Colleagues are different. If you've never had them, you will find it difficult to understand the concept. (I have heard similar remarks made about the concept of comradeship in the Armed Forces.)

It may well be that the first time you come across them is when you enter the teaching profession. (It would be the same in any profession.) When you do, you must learn, quickly, to appreciate them. They deserve to be treated with a level of correctness and formality which is easily visible. In the case of teaching, particularly in the presence of pupils. Finally, if you become half a teacher, you learn, and again quickly, that theirs is the respect which you most want, and work hardest to win.

Not parents. Not headmasters. Not even pupils. Of course their esteem comes high in the list of desirables, but not as high as that of colleagues or – to use the word (of which I am wary) for the, I think, only time in this book – peers. They are the people who understand best what you do, and are therefore the best judges of it.

I once heard a sharp example of this idea expressed neatly when a primary school headmaster offered an appreciation to accompany a leaving present to his school secretary: 'Only Mrs. Wade knows what I do, and only I know what Mrs. Wade does.'

* * * * * *

One very human desire – or at the very least aspiration – is thanks. Thanks are an important ingredient of civilisation. When we draw up lists of basic good manners that we hope to teach our children, it is arguable that 'thank you' might come slightly higher than 'please'.

We all like 'thank you'. From the basic two words and the Christmas boxes to retirement encomiums and the long service and good conduct medals. My impression is that they are not quite so thick on the ground in teaching as elsewhere. Or rather that they do not come very quickly. (I am talking about pupils now.) This is probably not because of rank ingratitude; rather because of thoughtlessness and eagerness to move on. When I completed my basic training in the Army, I was grateful in a circuitous sort of way to my drill sergeant, whose stern methods had made a platoon out of us. But it was the end of the passing-out parade, we had just survived the sternest ten weeks of our young lives, and our leave passes were burning a hole in our pockets. I doubt if any of us thought or stopped to turn back and shake his hand. And, professional that he was, he would have understood that.

Sixth-formers, having, at long last, come to the end of thirteen years of education and tottered out of their last examination, put shaking the dust of school from their shoes at the top of their agenda; so they do not always surge back into the classroom to give a vote of thanks to 'Sir' or 'Miss'. Much less pupils of primary age. (This is yet another generalisation. Some of them do indeed say thank you, often very graciously, and this is always much valued.)

They are not ungrateful; they just have so many more things on their mind. They have come through one mighty long world and out the other side; they are eager to step into another. They would be unusual if they were not.

What you will more likely get instead is a casual meeting in the street twenty or thirty years later, with a parent (maybe even greying at the edges), with a family in tow, who will remind you of something you said or did all those years ago, and for which they have been grateful ever since.

It is well worth waiting for, because it is mature, considered comment, and you can be sure that it is genuine. If it were not, they wouldn't have taken the trouble to stop and say.

Put simply, if you want thanks, you may have to wait quite a long time for it, and you can't guarantee it even then.

* * * * * *

One of the sins we are commonly guilty of is to make assumptions and generalisations about occupations of which we know little or nothing. Surgeons? Ugh! All that blood. Navvying? All those holes in the road. Dentists? Ugh again! Looking down people's throats. Teaching? God – all that marking. And non-stop noisy kids.

All these sweeping statements do still have their share of truth. We would never get used to all that blood, but surgeons do, in between doing a lot of other things we know next to nothing about. We could not survive a whole week digging holes, but navvies manage to, in between their many other tasks. Dentists looking down people's throats have a lot more to worry about than the nation's uvulas. It's a question of your knowledge and your point of view. If you don't know much, you don't see much.

What I am saying in a laborious sort of way is that there is much more variety in other people's jobs than we see in a casual, uninterested glance.

Yes, teaching has its boring parts – the cliché parts – like every other job. Every teacher has to stiffen the sinews and summon up the blood when faced with six piles of exercise books or a couple of hundred exam papers or a week of invigilation of public exams. But common sense and a couple of minutes' thought dictate that, if that was all teaching was about, it would not attract many applicants.

Teaching, truth be told, has as much variety as any other job, though it may come in unexpected, and sometime unwelcome, forms.

For example, we can't all like every pupil we get, much less every class. If, when we look for the first time at our new timetable at the beginning of the autumn term, we find we are landed with the notorious 4K, we have little alternative but to lump it. (Teaching involves rather a lot of lumping it.) But unless things have gone very awry, we can trust our head of department not to have given us a class that he knows we can't handle. On the contrary, he could well have given us 4K because he had judged that we are now competent enough to cope, or he trusts us enough to imply that, by giving us 4K, he knows he will not have to worry about them for a year. Either way, it's a sort of compliment.

If you are really dedicated (and we hope that at least some of you are), you can maybe follow the lofty advice to treat every problem as an opportunity. If you can, bully for you; you are on the way to becoming the ideal teacher. But if you are mortal like the vast majority of us, take heart; whatever happens, even if they don't learn much that year, the chances are that you will. So it's not all debit.

The same thing applies to individual pupils. In the whole pupil body, rest assured that there will be some variety. Ask any teacher with a dozen years of experience; he or she will regale you with details – complimentary, wry, painful, despairing – of particular boys and girls who have burned themselves into the memory, for any of scores of reasons. You will have variety all right.

And they won't all turn out to be success stories. Do not beat your breast too much about them. Yes, of course, it may have been partly your fault, but at least you know – and you admit – that you didn't get through to Patrick or Angela or whoever it was. You do at least *know* that you didn't do well. You have to live with failure. All artists paint *some* rotten pictures (they are lucky; they can throw them away). Some film stars make bad pictures, and there isn't much they can do about that; it's in the can. If a pupil leaves school disgusted, disillusioned, or furious, well, he has at least gone. You have to worry only about the memory, and you can at least chalk it up to experience. Which you learn from. Every experience has its uses.

Bear in mind too the old adage about the glass being

half-empty or half-full. Look at the whole glass and the whole contents. Teaching is like everything else – being a priest and saving souls; being a games coach and winning the cups; being a door-to-door salesman and filling your order-book; you win some and you lose some. You would be a very rare teacher if you lost them all. If it really were that bad, you would have tumbled to it quite early on (let us hope you are not stupid as well as woefully incompetent); you would have sat down to do some pretty stern thinking. You would have 'considered your position'.

Variety or no variety, time and again, one finds oneself coming back to the timeworn advice which, we hope, will get you through. Its ubiquity does not necessarily weaken the currency. Stop worrying. Remember you're all right. Just get on and do it. Put the bat to the ball. Learn the lines. Tell the tale. Mark the damn books.

* * * * * *

Guess what. One thing leads to another. The more you do what I suggested in the last paragraph, the more Brownie points you collect, naturally. But collecting them involves effort. In other words you get tired.

Well, don't you get tired doing anything else? Yes, of course you do. If you spend too many hours in the day doing it, you do. Most of my working days have been spent teaching, so I don't know much about other jobs. But I imagine that the same idea would apply.

But maybe teaching is a little different. Not unique, but different. Everybody complains about their job from time to time, but I get the impression that, in complaints about the process of teaching, tiredness seems to figure more than it does elsewhere. And it isn't just physical.

It was certainly the case in my own teaching years. Sooner or later – and probably sooner – you come up against the phenomenon of *chronic* fatigue. I have known of young teachers, otherwise admirably suited to the profession, who have left because of it.

I would venture to say that it is a rare young teacher who does not come up against it. And he or she will have to evolve some kind of strategy to deal with it. If he doesn't want a wretched life, that is.

I am not an educational psychologist, or any other kind of psychologist. I can not pontificate about the medical aspects of chronic fatigue; my only authority for talking about it is the fact that I fell victim of it. All I can do is to reassure young teachers (and maybe middle-aged ones too) that it is common to get it, and it is no disgrace to suffer from it. And perhaps my own experience of it may provide assistance, or at least a dash of moral support, to other sufferers.

For a start, try and learn to recognise it. It is more than a mere yawn or two. If problems start to loom larger, hours begin to last longer, Friday relentlessly slides further away, naughty pupils become naughtier, surprises catch you more unawares, tempers grow shorter, and all the rest, you are not losing your grip and becoming a worse teacher. Well, you are slipping slightly, but before you descend into the Slough of Despond, look at each of these symptoms, and see what can be done about each of them. It usually helps to reduce a problem to its component parts. (Not the wall, remember, but the bricks.)

Work out how one of them can trigger another. Try and detect where the downward spiral, the vicious circle, begins. You know you are tired. Work out why. Once you can get a handle on the causes, you are on the way to creating some treatment.

Some of this procedure can prove to be surprisingly simple. Along the lines of the riddle about: 'What happens to an elephant when it rains? Answer: it gets wet.' 'Why are you tired? Because you are not getting enough sleep.' I am not suggesting that it is all as simple as that, but it's a fair place at which to start. Ask yourself the obvious questions first.

Here are some other possibles. Are you eating well, sensibly, and regularly? (Dare I suggest it: are you drinking 'sensibly'?) Are simple frustrations getting you down more quickly than they did a month or two ago? Are you expecting too much from yourself? (Try asking a colleague, or a friend who can be relied on to tell you the truth. He can see the fraying at the edges better than you can.) How good is your social life these days? Are you finding excuses to stay behind at the end of the day for 'extra-mural activities' in order to avoid a chaotic family tea-time?

Are you taking on too many of these activities (never mind the family) because you are too much of a willing horse, or a push-over for a persuasive argument? Or you just like too many things. You can often see this going on with pupils too. (You can't do everything.) Because of a working day that you have allowed to provide too few breaks, are you loading yourself down with marking to take home? Any teacher can easily add to the list.

Once some problems have been identified like this, some curative strategies at once suggest themselves. Don't stay late up watching TV; drink something nice before going to bed. Don't join too many clubs. Learn to say 'No'.

(Politely of course.) Ease off on the carbohydrates. Don't bite off huge chunks of a problem; don't expect to knock it off all at once. Little and often. Tackle it when you feel ready and it's your idea; don't put it off till it looms over you like a tsunami wave. Intervals, changes, breaks. Think ahead and try to evolve systems, habits, rituals, however tiny. It means you are in control; you have arranged it.

Don't just plan the lesson; plan the morning as well. The afternoon. The day, the week, the whole term. Learn to pace it. You have to keep going for thirty-five weeks, and they have a right to expect a level of consistency and efficiency from you right up to the end of it. Thought. Planning. Control. If you have to shed some luggage on the way, in the shape of ambitions or bright ideas, so be it; it is important that you get to the end of thirty-five weeks with some semblance of order – and grip.

Teachers are busy souls. They have to be. They have to learn to cope. I once spent a week in a local factory, 'observing'. I think it was a scheme which was intended to give local teachers a chance to learn how the rest of the population earned their living; to deposit teachers, if only for a week, in the 'real world'.

I spent the whole of Friday in the Finance Department. My abiding impression is the urgency with which the staff who calculated, administered and distributed end-of-week wages (or salaries or 'remuneration' or whatever they were called) emphasised, stressed, and generally drove home their point. (This was before the more modern techniques of the digital transfer of money.) It was of absolutely paramount importance, they said, that all employees received every conceivable piece of information, and coinage, relative to their salary entitlement, in full, regularly, and on time. If they didn't, there would be a mutiny. It was far more important than even the Managing Director's new coffee-making machine. Without any question, this was the Deadline of the Week.

I duly frowned in concentration, and nodded very significantly. But the thought running through my head at the time was: This Finance Department is making a meal of one deadline every week. There are countless thousands of teachers, particularly secondary teachers, who, in a routine timetable, have up to eight deadlines to meet *every day*. They have to be ready, with lesson notes, class lists, marksheets, text-books (perhaps equipment too), homework marked, and a hefty dollop of energy, anything up to *thirty times a week*.

There will be plenty of times when teachers (who, as I have been at pains to show, are human) feel the pressure, and in low moments can fall prey to doubts about their efficiency. This is the time when they need a lift.

A possible suggestion is this. Look ahead (after all, you know what's coming) and try to arrange that, somewhere along the line, you manufacture, secure, arrange, provoke, a success. Never mind how humble – a clear, discernible success. You have done something; you have an achievement to chalk up. Something went dead right. It does wonders for the morale. It's not bad for class morale either. They quite like 'Sir' to be a winner.

I once taught, encouraged, and induced a very backward twelve-year-old boy (who was possibly autistic as well) to stand up in front of the whole class and recite the alphabet. Just the alphabet, nothing else. He got a round of applause. All right, it was his triumph, not mine, but after several weeks of struggle, I had the rare pleasure of hearing a spontaneous round of applause in the classroom. That is a rare, cheerful noise, and it did me, and John, no end of good.

John gave a performance. Performances can take it out of you. John, bless him, had to do it only once. Teachers, I maintain, (and I have said so before in this book) give a performance every time they take a lesson.

That works out at just over a thousand performances a year. Not even West End actors do that. No wonder teachers can get tired. Next time someone tells you he thinks it's pretty easy, suggest that he tries it.

* * * * * *

There is space for one more observation. There are bound to be others I could have tacked on, but unless one is writing a reference book, there is no necessary virtue in aiming at an encyclopaedia. The seeker after wisdom wants strategic pinpoint aiming, not saturation bombing.

So, what thought could one profitably leave with you? I would plump for power. Consider power.

Teachers have power, and they like it.

Debut teachers enjoy being the centre of attention. It's good having young people around you who can respond well for the simple reason that you are quite close to them in age. If you find you are good at what you are doing, they will respond more. Like all power, it is heady stuff.

If you are experienced, we hope you have improved. You now know enough to be aware of how much influence you are having. That should make you watchful. You can trade on it, in order to enhance the effect of your teaching, but at all times keep a watchful eye on the vanity gauge. Or if you prefer, the conceit thermometer.

It is simple arithmetic: you are older. It is life: you have experience; they have not. Despite their capacity for cynicism, mischief, and sedition, they want what you've got. It's quite a useful trump card to carry up your sleeve. But remember what the man said about power corrupting.

22 Throwing the biscuit

Why are teachers never satisfied? Not because they are miseries, or gradgrinders, or pathological perfectionists. In fact it's a sort of sideways compliment; they think you are capable of doing just a little better.

The same principle applies here. You, the attentive reader, the dedicated practitioner, the willing learner, have shown enough patience to reach the end of the book. You have gathered up all the pearls of wisdom so liberally scattered before you; you have been fair-minded enough to accept the warnings, the reproofs, the criticisms, the recommendations. You have given credit where you think credit is due.

You are now primed, prepared, equipped, fully armed to face them, and to teach them right off the screen. You've done it; you've got it; you've cracked it. So they'd all better watch out.

You have indeed done well. You have induced them to listen to you. You have caught their interest. You have inspired their effort. You have inculcated good habits of work. You have kept them up to the mark. You have mastered the two techniques required – the carrot and the stick. You have steeled them to grapple with difficulties over an extended period. Best of all, they have succeeded; you, and they, are basking in the glow of glittering results.

Is that it? Not quite.

Well, they are pleased, aren't they? Oh, yes. But they need to know that you are pleased too. They need to know that you have noticed.

Like you, they are human (though there have probably been times along the way when you may have had your doubts). This is nothing to do with being young or a pupil; everybody needs to have their self-respect fed. Wanting approval is not just a touching little propensity of the young, like dimples. Everybody – everybody – is pleased to receive praise for their efforts and achievements.

Especially if it's public. Pride withers in silence and solitude. An audience doesn't half help. A gold medal in an empty, silent stadium would have somewhat less appeal. How do you do it in a classroom?.

A stadium and an audience usually do it by means of noise. You – the teacher – you can't carry around with you a stadium and an applause machine. You have to do it by other means. It is up to you to devise a way of conveying approval. It doesn't matter much how. But it must be done. Don't leave the job three-quarters finished. You have polished off the difficult part; you have inspired them to make the effort; you have made them want to gain your approval. You must – you *must* – show them that they have won it.

So there are two things that you have to get across – how to master the knowledge and technique to ensure that they succeed, and how to show your pleasure that they have done so. More, they must see that you appreciate what their success means to them. More still, you must show that their success *matters to you.*

Once again, this is where the trust comes in – that trust you have so carefully built. Persist, persuade, cajole, chase, even bark and growl, yes. But however much you push them, they must feel sure that you are on their side. Slave-driver maybe, but a slave-driver with a dash of soft centre. Show them that you know how hard they are trying.

Nor do you save the accolades for when the job is

done. That is important, of course it is. But praise matters even more beforehand, when they are struggling with it. Encourage, encourage, encourage, all the time. It doesn't matter if 90% of the job they hand in is rotten. The chances are that they know that already. (It is your job to cure it.) But you will know whether or not the effort was genuine.

If you spot that the other 10% is good – *and say so* – (maybe even explain *why* it's good) they'll be pleased – perhaps even thrilled to bits. They will cheerfully chalk up that 90% to experience. You have opened a way forward.

For the bright pupil, or the keen pupil, or the pupil with an educated, interested family, the way forward is open and clear all the time. It is just another job to be tackled and done. For many of the others, it is not so simple. They do not have same record of success to look back on. If the past looks a bit bleak, you as the teacher have to try and open a more attractive future.

You have to sell them on the idea that the effort has a fair chance of producing success. That is where the encouragement comes in. Which is why that promising 10% is such a useful tool in your armoury. It is up to you to find it, and exploit it.

Don't worry whether you are getting it across. If you are trying, it will show, just as their effort will show with you. They have been alive long enough to know that approval comes in a wide variety of guises. If you have got to know them, and they have got to know you (which again is up to you), it won't matter. Whether it is an illuminated scroll or an absent-minded grunt, it will count. They will understand. *But it has to be something.*

We all need recognition. Like everybody else, a pupil in

a classroom has a right to feel sure that the teacher knows he's there. Better still, that he knows the teacher appreciates what he's doing. When he's doing something wrong, and, more important, when he's doing something right. Not just now and then, or at the end of a job. Always. Any praise works, big or small, so long as they understand how you mean it.

If the relationship you have built is a good one, no progress or success is complete until 'Sir' or 'Miss' has said 'Bravo!'

THE END

www.ingramcontent.com/pod-product-compliance
Lightning Source LLC
LaVergne TN
LVHW052254070426
835507LV00035B/2545